Federico

Rico Lebrun
(1900-1964)

An exhibition of drawings, paintings
and sculpture organized for
the Los Angeles County Museum of Art
by Henry J. Seldis

With catalog essays by Mr. Seldis,
Art Editor, Los Angeles Times
and Dr. Peter Selz, Director,
University Art Museum, UC Berkeley

Copyright 1967
by the Los Angeles County Museum of Art

Printed in the United States of America

Library of Congress
Catalog Card Number 67-31098

Los Angeles County Museum of Art,
December 5, 1967 to January 14, 1968

Instituto Nacional de Bellas Artes,
Mexico, D.F.
February 15 to March 15, 1968

University of Arizona, Tucson,
April 15 to May 16, 1968

University of California, Berkeley,
June 17 to July 29, 1968

Seattle Art Museum,
August 29 to October 6, 1968

Oklahoma Art Center, Oklahoma City,
November 2 to December 15, 1968

National Collection of Fine Arts,
Washington, D.C.
February 15 to March 15, 1969

Lenders to the Exhibition

Estate of Rico Lebrun
Mr. and Mrs. Harry A. Altman, Los Angeles, California
Mr. and Mrs. Winslow Ames, Saunderstown, Rhode Island
Mrs. Donald B. Ayres, Jr., Newport Beach, California
Mrs. Donald Bear, Santa Barbara, California
Mrs. Morris D. Behrend, New York, New York
The Honorable and Mrs. William Benton, Southport, Connecticut
Dr. and Mrs. Albert S. Chase, Los Angeles, California
Miss Adele Clement, New York, New York
Mrs. Constance Lebrun Crown, Malibu, California
Mr. and Mrs. Sidney Deutsch, White Plains, New York
Mr. and Mrs. Ross R. DeVean, Riverside, California
Mr. and Mrs. Robert Eichholz, Washington, D.C.
Mr. and Mrs. Jack Elliott, Studio City, California
Mrs. Guenn Farington, Santa Barbara, California
Mr. and Mrs. M. F. Feheley, Toronto, Canada
Mr. Thomas A. Freiberg, Los Angeles, California
Dr. and Mrs. Milton M. Gardiner, Merrick, New York
Mr. and Mrs. Sumner Gerstein, Brookline, Massachusetts
Mr. and Mrs. Mayer Greenberg, Los Angeles, California
Mr. and Mrs. Joel Grey, New York, New York
Mrs. Muriel Harris, New York, New York
Mr. and Mrs. Melvin Hirsch, Beverly Hills, California
Mr. and Mrs. Leslie L. Johnson, Dayton, Ohio
Mr. and Mrs. Sidney S. Kingsley, New York, New York
Mr. and Mrs. David Lebrun, Malibu, California
Mr. and Mrs. Robert J. Levyn, Los Angeles, California
Dr. and Mrs. S. Lifschutz, New Brunswick, New Jersey
Professor and Mrs. Edwin H. Miller, Riverdale, New York
Mr. and Mrs. Albert Millman, South Orange, New Jersey
Miss Agnes Mongan, Cambridge, Massachusetts
Dr. Francisco Olsina, San Miguel de Allende, Mexico
Channing Peake, Beverly Hills, California
Mr. and Mrs. James Pinto, San Miguel de Allende, Mexico
Mr. and Mrs. William Ptaszynski, Goleta, California
Dr. and Mrs. Leo Rangell, Los Angeles, California
Mr. and Mrs. John Rex, Northfork, California
Selden Rodman, Oakland, New Jersey
Mr. and Mrs. Seymour J. Rubin, Washington, D.C.
Nathaniel Saltonstall, Boston, Massachusetts

Dr. and Mrs. Sylvan Schireson, Los Angeles, California
Miss Tanya Selz, New York, New York
Robert W. Service, Burbank, California
Dr. and Mrs. Mac L. Sherwood, Beverly Hills, California
Mr. and Mrs. Norton Simon, Los Angeles, California
Mrs. Otto L. Spaeth, New York, New York
Mr. and Mrs. Michael Straight, Washington, D.C.
Mr. and Mrs. David Thorne, Pasadena, California
Mr. and Mrs. Leonard Titleman, New York, New York
Mr. and Mrs. Bernard Warner, Los Angeles, California
Howard Warshaw, Carpinteria, California
Mr. and Mrs. Stuart Weaver, Jr., Los Angeles, California
Dr. and Mrs. Herman Weiner, Beverly Hills, California
Miss Shelley Wexler, New York, New York
Mr. and Mrs. Nick B. Williams. La Canada, California
Mr. and Mrs. James A. Wood, Riverside, California
Mr. and Mrs. Frank S. Wyle, Los Angeles, Calfiornia
Paul W. Zimmerman, Hartford, Connecticut

The Cleveland Museum of Art, Ohio
Corcoran Gallery of Art, Washington, D.C.
Cornell University, Ithaca, New York
Delphic Arts, New York, New York
Fogg Art Museum, Harvard University, Cambridge, Massachusetts
S. C. Johnson & Sons, Inc., Racine, Wisconsin
Lee Nordness Galleries, Inc., New York, New York
Los Angeles County Museum of Art, California
Metropolitan Museum of Art, New York, New York
Munson-Williams-Proctor Institute, Utica. New York
Museum of Modern Art, New York, New York
The North Carolina Museum of Art, Raleigh
Pennsylvania Academy of the Fine Arts, Philadelphia
Philadelphia Museum of Art, Pennsylvania
Santa Barbara Museum of Art, California
Silvan Simone Gallery, Los Angeles, California
University of Nebraska, Lincoln
Whitney Museum of American Art, New York, New York
Worcester Art Museum, Massachusetts
Yale University Art Gallery, New Haven, Connecticut

Acknowledgements

This catalog is dedicated to the memory of my dear friend
Donald Bear, founding director of the Santa Barbara
Museum of Art, whose support of Rico Lebrun and many other
West Coast artists was crucial in their development.

Without the wholehearted assistance of the artist's widow
Mrs. Constance Lebrun Crown and his son, David Lebrun,
this exhibition would not have been possible.

I wish to thank Director Kenneth Donahue of the Los Angeles
County Museum of Art, for keeping faith with the
commitment of his predecessor in inviting me to mount this
exhibition. My gratitude also to Dr. Peter Selz, an old friend and
welcome collaborator, who encouraged me in this venture
and contributed the essay on the *Genesis* mural in Pomona,
which would not have come into being without him.

I am indebted to Henry Hopkins for his supervision of the
entire project and for his sensitive installation, and to
Dorothe Curtis and Frieda Fall for their organizational assistance.

A special word of thanks to Helene Winer who compiled
the chronology and bibliography in this catalog and whose help
to me has been invaluable. My wife, Dr. Anna Bruni Seldis,
has been most helpful in providing translations of Rico Lebrun's
Italian writings and putting up with my preoccupation
during this venture.

Mr. and Mrs. Donald Winston and Mr. and Mrs. Frank Wyle
have made much appreciated financial contributions to the
exhibition. Teresa Parker of Jacques Seligman Gallery,
New York; Lee Nordness of the Nordness Galleries, New York
and Silvan Simone of the Simone Gallery, Los Angeles
have been most cooperative.

My conversations with Channing Peake, Howard Warshaw,
William and Teresa Ptaszynski, George Goyer and many
other of Lebrun's friends and associates provided important
insights into his life and work.

To the many individuals and institutions who have readily
agreed to the extended loans necessary for this traveling
exhibition we are especially grateful.

Finally, I wish to thank the directors of the participating
institutions, Sr. Jose Luis Martinez, Mr. William E. Steadman,
Dr. Peter Selz, Dr. Richard E. Fuller, Mr. Patrick Shannon
and Dr. David Scott for their enthusiasm regarding
this exhibition.   *H.J.S.*

Beyond Virtuosity

by Henry J. Seldis

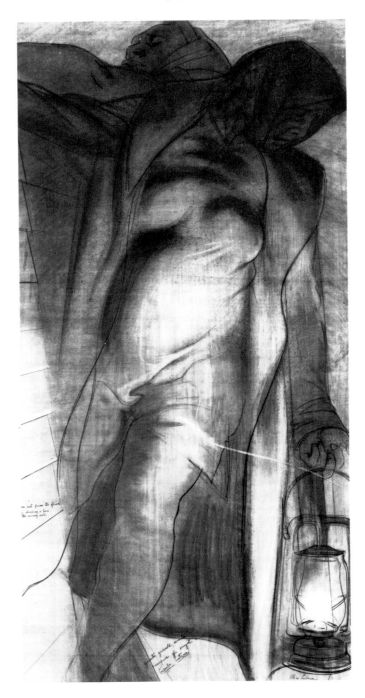

The tough and the tender are equally evident in the life and work of Rico Lebrun (1900-1964), an artist of eloquence and pertinence, who chose to comment on the continual crises of his time and of his being in a language that never lost its humanity yet transcended it in spirit and scale.

Detesting the illustrative as much as the geometrically abstract, Lebrun navigated between these two rocks at first with brilliant calculation and finally, with a poignant sense of liberation from all concerns with fame and fashion.

Although he was a virtuoso draftsman capable of every possible performance, Lebrun became determined to scare technique "... like a dog impassioned and imaginative incurring the anger of the hunter." As an impassioned observer of human beings this artist came to the realization that he could not "make them idiot creatures but august, frightful and elevated."

As a native Italian, Lebrun had an innate fascination with the tragic gesture. As a descendant of Spaniards, he knew the rhythms of cruelty as well as of love. As a resident American, he understood the pertinence of large scale and vast dimensions. As a poet, he rarely mistook shouting for eloquence.

The human figure was Lebrun's subject — a subject that he knew could never be explored fully. He approached it in terms of architecture, he entered it as one enters a landscape, he saw its epic meaning as well as its absurdities, he managed to consider its totality while loving its separate parts, he never considered it without being caught up in it. The human figure was at once the greatest sustenance and the greatest challenge that Lebrun found in his life of becoming an artist.

While the virtuosos of the ever changing styles of his time often managed to get away with nothing in their successful search for fame and fortune, Lebrun was largely denied such material rewards because he continued to struggle with fury and despair "to come by every means to terrible and sensible terms with the painting of the soul of my time."

War and murder, nuclear holocaust and calculated genocide were events that were central not only in Lebrun's life but in his work, while they remained peripheral in the art of most of his contemporaries who were no less conscious of the brutality of their time but were unwilling or unable to express it in figurative terms.

The creatures of darkness which constitute the common denominator of Lebrun's prolific outpouring are illuminated by a faith in both mankind and in painting which he had to wrest almost daily from his grave doubts about the world and his own role in it.

Painfully but mercilessly, Lebrun stripped himself of his own facility, of his fantastic native gifts. The macabre and the grotesque were more real to him than the ideal or the decorous. If he detested the clerical cant of the Catholic Church in which he was brought up and openly fought the Babbitts of organized religion, Lebrun never ceased to worship in the cathedral of the human form or to extoll the potentials of the human spirit.

Death and destruction are major ingredients in his art, but in the final analysis even a fragmentary and subjective survey of his work such as this, evokes an undeniable sense of affirmation. With it comes the realization that Lebrun's life and work have never yet been adequately explored and the recognition that in his very own very timely reinvention of Baroque form Lebrun had indeed found the very idiom needed to paint the soul of his time.

If Lebrun's anatomies seem monstrous at first, they take on quite another significance when we consider their poetic and symbolic meanings wrung from the pain and passion of the man who wrote:

I and they will die in the open air with blue shadows and membranes wrapping up internal organs finer than silk with nets of rubies and gold of bile. They are bodies made to speak aloud and in a low voice to God about the glories and miseries of a woman's womb and a man's belly. They have a tremendous hunger to reveal themselves as they are in a dream and not as they appear in life. There is a grave voice of lament that goes with all this.

But Lebrun's inevitable shout of triumph is heard in the very same letter to his life-long friend Mario Labocetta as he writes "I am finding a mouth like a burning pomegranate. When you kiss it, it makes you a painter."

Lebrun had no truck with the nonsense of "beautiful painting". Little by little he learned how to create much more with much less, and at the

very end of his life his golden hands finally belonged only to him.

His manner of working was obsessive, his most moving visions are revelatory. If they continue to be disturbing, it is our striving to deny our own disordered patterns that make them so. In his art Lebrun rejected the notion that we go to the chaos of nature to bring private order out of it. Instead he created a spiritual and plastic parallel of nature's multiplicity.

Much of his life Lebrun struggled against the facility of his own draftsmanship and the brilliant virtuosity which had brought him acclaim soon after he came to this country from his native Italy in 1924.

For all the consummate artistry of his early romantic drawings, for all the tragedy projected by the very best of his 1950 *Crucifixion* series, in the last decade of his life, Lebrun—an incisive force on young West Coast artists of the 1940's and 1950's — reached far beyond his own stylistic brilliance and trenchant plastic polemicism.

With the creation of the powerful *Genesis* mural at Pomona College (1960) and its preparatory works, Lebrun, whose prolific dynamism spilled over into teaching and writing, moved himself and the viewer from outside the anatomical and spiritual event which his work had held in focus right into the physical, psychological and spiritual arena of life and death.

The overwhelming accomplishment of Lebrun's drawings inspired by Dante's *Inferno* was due to the fact that this artist had come to the point where his undivided concern was to express himself primarily for his own fulfillment. Now ready to pursue his plastic and philosophical aims without regard for public acclaim or criticism (or for the lack of it), this most disciplined and inspired artist plunged into soul-baring improvisations and inventions of the first magnitude. The human image, always central to this masterly artist's work — once so clearly defined, so specifically linear in the Lebrun vision — became amorphous, fragmented and tactile.

By presenting us with majestic ruins of man's form, an essential and convincing humanism drives home to us his conviction that whatever physical, psychological and mortal tortures are inflicted on the human form, its innate dignity and the unfulfilled promise of the human spirit cannot be annihilated. It was the light of Lebrun's extraordinary intelligence and of his unflinching faith which gave us undeniable visions of the spirit triumphant.

As this artist used the tremendous structural, textural, and linear vocabulary at his command with utter abandon and frenzied compulsion, creating pictorial metamorphoses in which the boundaries between exterior and interior were demolished, his expression took more and more plastic form until, toward the very end of his life, he overcame his own agonies of dying to create some of the most moving and accomplished figurative sculptures produced in our time.

A substantial number of these sculptures (never before exhibited) and many of the drawings and paintings completed during the last five years of Lebrun's life (not widely shown outside his home territory) are included in this survey of the artist's work.

We are too close in time to Lebrun's monumental achievements to fully comprehend their magnitude or to explain adequately why these undeniable accomplishments evoked so much indifference as well as hostility. But by carefully selecting from his vast oeuvre, it is possible to demonstrate the contemporaneity as well as the timelessness of Lebrun's idiom.

Without relinquishing his lifelong stance against man's inhumanity to man, Lebrun, in his most telling works, concerned himself more with the conception of resurrection than with that of destruction, more with inner substance than with exterior appearance, more with the universal oneness of living things than with the essential isolation and mortal limitation of man's physical existence. The very compulsion of carrying his art into the third dimension in the face of his own death was a reiteration of his faith in the survival of spirit over body.

It is not really in Lebrun's metaphysical concept that we find his most distinctive contribution to his art and his time but in the way he transferred all he had ever learned of anatomy, of draftsmanship, of light and dark, of tradition and of invention into the three-dimensional medium so suitable for the ultimate expression of his esentially Baroque spirit.

Night

Rico Lebrun
1942

In many of the overtly amorphous images of his last period, Lebrun combines elements symbolic of indomitability with those of decay to show us that they are indeed two sides of the very same coin. In other drawings and sculpture completed shortly before his death, he comments sublimely on the interdependence between love and hate.

Beneath the anger and anguish found in much of the artist's work after he embarked on his momentous *Crucifixion* cycle in 1948, we find in his art a distinct note of affirmation. Even the most destroyed of his forms have their own kind of splendor and impassioned eloquence.

Central to all of his work — including the mural sketches of the 1930's, the Mexican collages of the 1950's and the seemingly brutal images of the 1960's — was Lebrun's sense of engagement and spiritual pertinence. From examples of fierceness and brutality he managed to wrest transcendent and convincing images that were no less contemporary for their reshaping of traditional forms.

The earliest works of the mature Lebrun, dating back to the 1940's, dealt with less tragic themes. Street musicians, clowns and peasant women were included as subject matter. Long before he perfected his own orchestrations on the human form, Lebrun talked to his friend and patron Donald Bear, the founding director of the Santa Barbara Museum of Art, about a major source of his art — the youthful memories of his native Naples. There is a considerable element of prediction in these 1947 comments, which in some measure could be used as comments on paintings and sculptures executed many years later:

On the sidewalk of a Mediterranean town I have seen a woman with child. She seemed the calm Venus of Athens, raked by hunger and love, and her flesh was a dense and eroded substance, of a color that seemed to permeate to the very bone. And I have felt that if I, as a painter, could some day master this, everything else belonging to my feeling of nature and art would follow. The cloud would be obedient and repeat the fierce mass of her tangled hair. The bay and the rock would be the answer to her pelvis and her flank. If this organic law were followed, there would not be possible any theatricism, or mirage, or collage, but the plastic drama moving and concluding in perfectly adequate space.

Rico Lebrun's oeuvre, especially its last phases, demands re-evaluation especially at a moment when the concept of poetry in its literal meaning is being rejected by many young artists. There is in Lebrun's organic poetry, in his unswerving pursuit of his own aims, in his own fight against the pitfalls of easy virtuosity, a heritage that could only have been left to us by an invincible spirit for whom tradition was a springboard and not a rear-view mirror.

Although Lebrun was not to enjoy the recognition that comes with a major one-man show until he was 40 years old, the years of his youth and early maturity, spanning radically different phases of life, are of considerable importance in attempting to understand the man and his work.

Born on December 10, 1900 in Naples, Lebrun was christened Federico. His father, a railroad official who enjoyed the company of intellectuals, was of French descent, while his mother had some Spanish ancestry.

Early Life

Although schooled for commerce, Lebrun thought of becoming a writer early in life. Significantly, he continued to write prolifically until his death. The almost daily writing — some of it aimed for publication, much of it more private in intent — parallels Lebrun's evolution as an artist. The strength and clarity of his verbal expression was also the foundation for his brilliant teaching abilities. Many of his games with letters, words and even languages represented imaginative juxtapositions very close in nature to the structural juggling of form found in his pictures.

At the age of 14 he was graduated from the National Technical School in Naples. Three years later he concluded his schooling at the National Technical Institute. He was immediately conscripted into the Italian Army. At the time of the 1919 Armistice he returned home to finish his tour of military service in the Navy where a superior officer noticed his capabilities as a draftsman and encouraged him to attend drawing classes at the Naples Academy of Fine Arts at night. Repelled by the pedantic methods of teaching practiced there, Lebrun spent much time in the museums of Naples studying and copying the Seicento masters. In 1920 and 1921, the young artist

also worked with the fresco painters Albino and Cambi.

"The few adult painters I knew at that time were all engaged in a form of impressionism which I could not reconcile with either the tone or the character of the life around me. The adopted confetti color ill suited the carnal and tangible quality of the town, which in fact only Baroque masters of Southern Italy had previously understood," Lebrun recalled in the autobiographical notes that appeared in the book on his drawings published by the University of California Press in 1961.

A 20th Century version of the Baroque notion informs all of Lebrun's major works. It is not a reflection of 17th Century mannerisms but an innate consciousness of the irresistible movement of vital forces. Like his ancestors, Lebrun was intoxicated by the ferment of life within and outside himself and never tired of trying to grasp the continuous, irresistible movement which creates time and is created by time. Like the masters of the Italian Baroque — but in contemporary terms — Lebrun hated the narrow prison of form which prevents life from taking everything along with it. He strove to express inner and exterior realities greater than himself, realities which in their irrepressible development burst through the boundaries of reason and the contours of draftsmanship.

Having attained a professional level of draftsmanship, largely through teaching himself, Lebrun decided to make art his life and successfully sought employment as a designer and supervisor in a major stained glass factory in 1922. Two years later the artist came to the United States when the factory opened a new branch in Springfield, Illinois where he was employed as a foreman.

At the expiration of his one year contract, Lebrun fled this provincial atmosphere and went to New York to establish himself as a commercial artist. His work was soon sought by major magazines like *The New Yorker* and *Vogue* who paid highly for his sketches and vignettes. During his first year in New York he married Portia Novello, herself a successful designer. Within five years, Lebrun had become one of the most highly paid magazine artists in New York but he grew increasingly dissatisfied with the topical and temporary nature of such work and devoted an increasing amount of time to work that he felt to be more creative and permanently meaningful.

In 1927 and 1928, Lebrun visited Italy. Having decided towards the end of 1930 to try to make his way as a creative artist, even if it meant putting aside his lucrative New York career, Lebrun again departed for a year and a half stay in Italy where he obtained a studio on the Via Margutta near the fresco painter Galimberti with whom he pursued his mural studies. It was in Rome that he met the painter Louis Rubenstein who, on a Harvard Fellowship, was also studying fresco technique with Galimberti. Among the trips the two young artists took was one to Orvieto where Lebrun was deeply impressed with the Signorelli murals which he was later to study at length and actually copy, taking advantage of scaffolding that had been erected for restoration purposes.

Among the indelible experiences made possible to the artist by his repeated visits to his native land were the discovery of the distinctive powers of Caravaggio, Uccello, Michelangelo and Orcagna; the architectural purity and artistic riches of the Campo Santo in Pisa; the sculptural outpourings of Bernini and the rediscovery of the Neapolitan Seicento masters.

Although Lebrun's visits to Italy diminished with time and became sporadic later in his life, the artist could never separate his innermost thoughts and feelings from his Italianate being. Nearly forty years after he first came to live in the United States, his writings and pictorial concepts were largely verbalized in Italian although his remarkable erudition had long been transferred also to his adopted tongue.

Whoever is to explore Lebrun's life and work more fully than this condensed catalog permits, will have to pay close attention to the artist's highly complex thoughts and contradictory feelings about Italy which haunted him throughout his life. While his art was to evolve into a powerful idiom here in America, I share the view of those who regard him essentially as a European artist.

In January 1933, Lebrun returned to New York from his extended sojourn in Italy and rented a studio on Banks Street. He joined Rubenstein, first at Harvard and then in New York, in fresco experiments. A joint mural venture of theirs was executed on

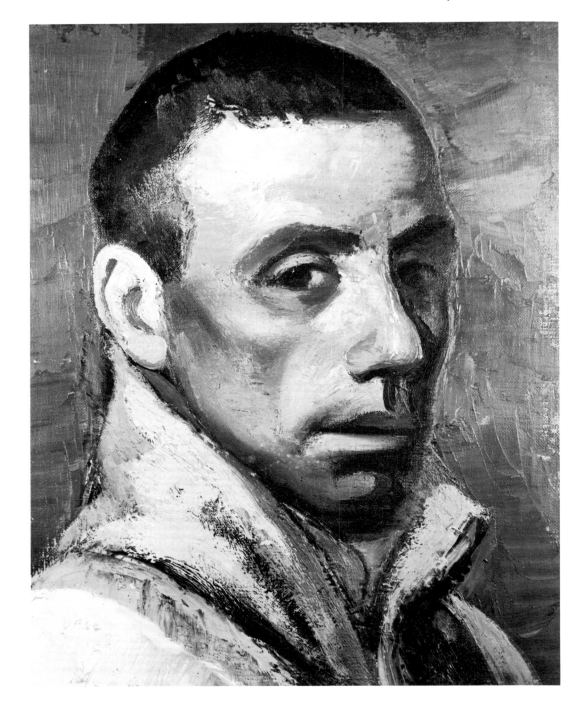

the walls of the top floor of Harvard's Fogg Museum. It was later covered up. In his studio Lebrun prepared his first monumental project — the cartoons for a *Story of the Mines* mural. Submitted with his application for a Guggenheim Foundation Fellowship, they won him the grant. With these funds in hand Lebrun returned to Orvieto where he spent many weeks in studying and tracing the Signorelli frescoes in the Cathedral. Meanwhile he had approached Works Progress Administration (WPA) with a scheme for a large mural cycle to be painted in a federal building. He also was invited to join the faculty of the Art Students League of New York.

Returning to New York in 1936, after the completion of his study trip to Europe, Lebrun embarked on his dual assignments as a WPA muralist and Art Students League teacher. Working voraciously in the New York Post Office Annex, Lebrun, with the help of artist-assistants Channing Peake and Gridley Barrows (both former students of "Luigi" Rubenstein), Lebrun began work on a gigantic fresco on the theme *River Flood*. He also received a renewal of his Guggenheim grant.

After two years of intensive work on the mural, a conflict arose between the artist and the WPA, forcing abandonment of the wall paintings which were covered over later. At the same time Lebrun was faced with the breakup of his first marriage. Disillusioned with New York because of these circumstances, Lebrun sought to move to California where Peake and his wife Katy and her parents, Mr. and Mrs. Max Schott, were eager to help him to a new start. Just before leaving New York he received his first invitation to the important 1938 Whitney Museum Annual.

Move to California

Shortly after coming to California, Lebrun joined the faculty of the Chouinard Art Institute in 1939. A year later he met Donald Bear, the dynamic young director of the Denver Art Museum who had come to Santa Barbara to be the founding director of that city's art museum then in its planning stages. In this brilliant man Lebrun found a friend and admirer who was to be his foremost champion until Bear's untimely death in 1953. It was Bear who brought Lebrun's work to the attention of leading curators, critics and

dealers, who organized the first important Lebrun show at the Santa Barbara Public Library's Faulkner Gallery and who invited Lebrun to become his museum's artist-in-residence in 1944.

Santa Barbara was the place of Lebrun's wedding in 1940 to Elaine Leonard, divorced wife of the painter Jon Corbino. That year Lebrun became active at the Walt Disney Studios where he taught animation and lectured on anatomy. He played a central role in devising the articulations for Disney's *Bambi*. His cinematographic experiences were to be very influential on his later work.

Through Bear, Lebrun's drawings and paintings, by then very powerful and accomplished, came to the attention of the Museum of Modern Art Curator Dorothy Miller who invited his work into her *Americans 1942* exhibition. That year Lebrun left Santa Barbara for New Orleans where he taught for a year at Sophie Newcomb College. He then returned to New York where he remained until December 1944 when Bear invited him to be artist-in-residence in Santa Barbara. He held this position for over two years with a brief interim of teaching at the Colorado Springs Fine Arts Center where he took Boardman Robinson's place in the spring of 1945.

Although Lebrun had performed prolifically as a draftsman and painter for nearly 20 years before first coming to California, it would not be exaggerated to date the emergence of his distinctive visual language as occurring somewhere in the late 1930's.

His dealings with the human figure were based on traditional precedent but they always reflected deep currents of contemporary life in symbolic terms. Not only had Lebrun absorbed the tenets of the Italian Renaissance and Baroque masters but he had delved through his intense interest in Picasso, into the structural experiments of Cezanne and into the agonizingly expressive notions of Grünewald's *Isenheim Altar*. By ancestral and temperamental inclination he had also become deeply involved in the idioms of the great Spaniards, especially El Greco, Zurbàran and Goya.

The beggars, cripples, harlequins and clowns that people Lebrun's work of the early 1940's are not only projections of these predilections but they are, as Bear pointed out in an early talk about Lebrun's work, "...a vehicle of criticism, deeply rooted in the

knowledge that even in the degradation of mental and physical despair there is still an intense significance in all fragments of life and feeling."

Having come to the point where he understood that nothing is established, everything is allowed in art, he consciously set himself a disciplinary problem in the form of his super-realistic still lifes that he called "my Spanish exercises." These remarkable paintings, based on his admiration of the Spanish still life masters, also served as an antidote to a series of moribund experiments in surrealism which were mostly destroyed by the artist.

An impassioned hunter and hiker, Lebrun began spending much time in the ranchlands of the Santa Ynez Valley near Santa Barbara. Soon he became engrossed not only in the plant life that he observed, sketched and imbued with his own bristling spirit but also in the architecture, color and symbolic potential of farm machinery. These are among his most powerful images and represent one of the very few extended periods in Lebrun's oeuvre when he departed from his preoccupation with the figure — though only superficially.

"Perhaps I moved away from the figure but not from anatomy," he was to write 15 years later. "The instruments were vertebral, scapular, joined, and the damn flesh color was now chrome green and yellow with rust. And the steel blue machines were supine, burnt and standing, crowned by light and posies. Yes, that's when I really began to reason with the figure — when it wasn't there."

His powerful interpretations of axles, ploughs, harrows and wagon wheels, elevated to a fervor and intensity that were mystical and poetic were the forerunners to the many works in which he was able to raise the character of the object at hand to the power of religious intensity. And it is in these farm implement paintings that Lebrun began closing in on his stated aim to have "...analysis and synthesis succeed each other as two beasts of the same function..." From here on he was continually striving to move from the particular to the general.

"Now the farm machinery had a quality of opened and colored structure, exactly what I had been looking for," Lebrun wrote in his *Drawings* book, "Here I found expression in the new sense I needed. The expression was the structure; the interval, the

span, was the physiognomy and the countenance. The machinery had square eyes of cobalt and ribs of cadmium red. The open works of the tractor were organs with clangor of orange blood; in the intervals of the open cage, in the furrow of the groin, sprouted the erect, green hair of the buttercup and the sage. The seeding and planting machines were made in the likeness of the locust and the mantis — savage, alert, predatory. The disk harrows were vetebrate; so was the bone-white, upright structure of the axle and wheel.

"It was here that I also found the world of color that I understand best—color which is the story of the object. A red, damaged and made partciular by use; the conditional, the related; the blaze made living and pertinent by sustained function — not the insipid, abstract birthday card, but the temperature chart of fevers and bleedings and rain and droughts."

In the *Farm Implements* series Lebrun opened a vein that was to be mined further by him during the tremendous undertaking of his *Crucifixion* cycle. In these germinal Santa Barbara paintings he made sure that all the objects in his compositions projected an emotional impact intrinsic to his own reaction rather than to the object's appearance.

Crucifixion Cycle

A link between the *Farm Implements* series and works in the *Crucifixion* cycle is constituted by the Whitney Museum's glowing *Wood of the Holy Cross* painting, dated 1948. Here we have a mixture of nonrepresentational colors and shapes with a few recognizably representational fragments: the mocking sign that was nailed to the Cross, the shafts of wood, the shroud. These serve to locate the subject. The persuasiveness of this work derives from the painter's ability to fuse these elements into an abstract design. The feelings of awe, tragedy and mystical experience evoked by this large panel are products of the suggested motion of colored shapes beneath the smooth black surface and of the balance of unequal forces of color and texture.

Critic Jules Langsner, a perceptive observer and incisive commentator of Lebrun's mature efforts, commented that with his bravura performance in creating the myriad drawings and scores of paintings of the *Crucifixion* cycle "Lebrun essayed to restore the

Lebrun 1947

power of dramatic eloquence to visual expression at a time when artists were increasingly occupied with marginal personalia."

"There came a time when I needed a subject, a theme, which could be put through successive illustrative variations, as a break from the self-centered procedure into which events and personal reverses had cornered me," Lebrun wrote in *Drawings*.

"The choice was a natural one. When I abandoned in my youth, with a sudden revulsion, some things related to my former faith that I could not properly understand, I abandoned at the same time what that faith had of sustenance and clarity. Now as an outcome of the war years, images related to the Crucifixion began to crowd in upon me in chains of ideas — not scattered thoughts but as rosary, as it were, of meditation. In a way, they were like a commentary on the nature of the Cross, the implements, the actors."

Surely his choice of theme was also related to his deep-rooted concern for the architecture of abstraction and to his penchant for the symbolic drama. Through more than 200 drawings and paintings, Lebrun created a polyptych of great fascination. At the completion of the series, inspired by a particular wall space in the old Los Angeles County Museum and aided and encouraged by his students at Jepson School, he painted the gigantic *Crucifixion Triptych*, now permanently installed at Syracuse University. Actually it depicts the Deposition. Unfortunately its very size and its location within the giant exhibition took away from many of the paintings of the entire series which in the judgement of many critics, including my own, are superior to the very quickly executed summation which suffered from being essentially an afterthought.

Although Lebrun's plan to make a filmed version of the *Crucifixion* cycle was never adequately realized, it is evident that he saw each painting and drawing as an individual frame on a reel, complete in itself but only fully realizable in visual relation to all the other images. His cinematographic intent also had much to do with the basically monochromatic emphasis of the series.

Dr. William R. Valentiner, the distinguished art historian who headed the County Museum's Art Division at the time Curator James Byrnes prepared the enormous Lebrun exhibition in 1950 (also shown at the De Young Museum, San Francisco), understood that unlike other American artists who had grappled with the horrors of war which had entered deeply into the American mind, Lebrun took cognizance of the element of rebirth contained in every decay.

In describing the vast fields of destruction portrayed through Lebrun's *Crucifixion* series, the late Dr. Valentiner wrote:

It is as if the lava of Mount Vesuvius, in which neighborhood the artist was reared, had covered the green lawn of the earth: smashed tanks, battered soldiers, massacre of the innocents, the weeping Mary, Magdalen tearing her hair, split trees, rotten roots and impaired ploughs, skeletons of horses neighing as though alive, men awakening from dreams of horror and despair, animals protected by armor in a fearful defensive mechanized world. These are the tragic subjects of his world of depersonalized ghosts.

But these destroyed and destroying creatures form a beautiful abstract pattern in the moment of their change from life to death, reflecting glowingly the new life which generates out of mortal agony.

Lebrun's astonishing, multifaceted comments on a sacrosanct theme are a prime example of his Baroque urgency to transcend all physical and psychological boundaries. The result of his immense concentration demonstrates the validity of his conviction that painting achieves transcendent power when it encompasses timeless human drama by means of the enduring human figure. It is not the artist's masterly handling of anecdotal devices that marks this series as a revival of visual eloquence but rather his insistence to force to the utmost all plastic means accessible to the contemporary artist.

The agonal emphasis of this vast project demonstrated vividly Lebrun's affliction by "…the meridianal temperament with all its burdens, with all its tumultuous contradictory behavior, and particularly the terrific sense of psychic mimicry we have. We respond to spectacle, we respond to disaster, we respond to happiness with a terrific amount of élan. I mean we are exaggerated in that we really participate."

Major paintings and important drawings from the *Crucifixion* series have found their way into a great number of important public and private collections. The controversial *Triptych* was exhibited in the stairwell of the Museum of Modern Art some years before it was acquired by Syracuse University.

Tragedy had also entered Lebrun's own life in 1946 with the death of his wife Elaine, which eventually triggered his move from Santa Barbara to Los Angeles where he joined the faculty of the newly formed Jepson Art Institute in 1947. Shortly before launching his *Crucifixion* cycle, Lebrun married Constance Johnson, the vivacious daughter of Pasadena architect Reginald Johnson, whose support and active collaboration in his professional life sustained the artist until his premature death. Soon after their marriage, Lebrun adopted his wife's son David to whom he was a devoted and inspiring parent.

Having finished nearly three years on a single theme, Lebrun, who had become director at Jepson Art Institute, turned to a joyously diverting task by executing designs for the ballet *Circo de España*, created by his friend, the great dancer Carmelita Maracci. It was a fitting prelude to his first trip to Mexico — a country with which he was to have ever more binding ties for the rest of his life. Having become established as a leading figurative painter in New York as well as on the West Coast since his first one-man show at the Julien Levy Gallery in 1944, Lebrun also became the recipient of numerous major awards and was included in many major invitational exhibitions for the following 20 years.

More than a decade after the completion of his cycle, Lebrun was to return to the Crucifixion theme with a far greater sense of immediacy than can be found in the carefully wrought works of the 1951 exhibitions which brought him to international attention for the first time.

Mexican Venture

After the enormous effort of completing the *Crucifixion* series, Lebrun felt the need for "a retreading, a refueling." Drawn to Mexico by its Latin characteristics and Baroque propensities — central also to the Mexican muralist movement — Lebrun accepted a teaching position at the Instituto Allende, San Miguel de Allende, where he taught in 1953 and 1954.

It proved to be a sort of homecoming. Lebrun's personality as well as his work always seemed somewhat hemmed in by the impassive conventions and the impersonal cosmopolitanism of Los Angeles. If there is a vast difference between Neopolitans and Mexicans, they nevertheless share the gusto and passion which Lebrun called "the hunger to be alive."

"In Mexico, in a savage and grand way, I found again things I knew from the land of my birth," Lebrun recalled in *Drawings*. "The same force seems to shape the face of the landscape and humans alike. I am thinking particularly of the volcanic land and the mountain plateaus of both countries. A fractured quality reveals the outer and inner surface of the land and beings at once.

Over and above the surface of the picturesque is the story of colored form with numberless footnotes of phenomenal accidents, bearing the signs of vicissitude, the anticlinical, the acceptance of ravages without paliative of plaster or explanatory consolations. Even the new walls have this obsessive insistence from pebbles to boulders as a petrified explosion. And the new colors are only a transparent skin over the organic body of structure you can easily guess and read through."

Light and color entered Lebrun's work in Mexico more than ever before. In his Mexican period Lebrun attempted to describe the transitory path of figures contained by landscape and of light altering and modifying both. He did not pursue the successive effects of light in a day, as did the Impressionists, nor the mechanical faceting of a disassembled body, as did the Cubists, but he strove to fuse the sum total of remembered and fleeting sensations into monumental images.

Although he continued to make a large number of ink drawings, some with biting satirical intent, the most important contribution made to his vocabulary came through his experimentations in collage — a medium in which true changes can be made spontaneously and through which he could evolve a total form, changing from figure to figure, in one composition. Through collage the artist found a new way of transforming the organic quality

of nature by tapping the image on different levels.

The monumental collages Lebrun created in Mexico (most of which had to be disassembled) consisted of cutouts which could be laid out on the studio floor where figural intentions could be discovered among shapes derived from street gestures, fleeting forms colored with aniline dye, flickering candle light, shadow patterns on a wall or a net covered plate of meat suggesting the anatomy of a head. Critic Donald Goodall observed astutely that during the Mexican interim Lebrun came to regard "…the picture as a habitat in which events occur but whose visual configuration is not to be interrupted by the gesticulations of a particular event."

During Lebrun's stay in San Miguel he managed to invigorate his spirit and his idiom to such a degree that it was to sustain him even as his return to Los Angeles brought his focus of attention back to agonizing themes. Rarely was Lebrun's creativity more spirited than in the most vivid of his Mexican pictures.

Towards Synthesis

James Thrall Soby characterizes Lebrun as "…a maverick to whose lonely ear violence speaks with particular urgency. The more distraught charades of our civilization have appealed to him especially." Just as he had turned his attention to the West's slaughterhouses a decade earlier, Lebrun began, upon his return to Los Angeles in 1956, to deal with the carnage of Buchenwald and Dachau, his traumatic engagement with these events having been renewed by photographic documentation of the gruesome death camps which then came to his attention. He sought the authenticity of brute fact as the raw materials for his commentaries.

"Yet, after having gone through days of absorbed and almost hallucinatory recording of these awesome fragments, I remember wanting to brush the whole thing away from me: the draftsman made their sight unbearable to me as a man: a just price to pay," Lebrun records in his book.

But his increased ability to tap the image on different levels towards a transformation of organic quality which resulted from his Mexican collage experimentations helped him solve a seemingly overwhelming psychological and plastic problem.

After having made lucid drawings based on the horrendous photographs until they became unbearable, Lebrun recalled that "…the mind drifted for a while and then remembered the upheaval of the spent furnace with fragments, islands here and there, of what had been the living body. Going to work again, I painted several versions, the truest being the ones in which I could not name the islands—pelvis, skull, whatever they had been."

In the best examples from this series Lebrun managed to fulfill his aim of changing what is disfigured into what is transfigured. Perhaps it was the very brutality of the subject he chose to interpret and the actual physical aversion with which he was filled while poring over the photographic documentation of genocide which gave final impetus to his long emergent desire to rid himself of the basically decorative virtuosity of draftsmanship on which his early fame had rested.

With this deliverance from facility a shifting of forms took place—based on an imaginative equivalent of the physical shuffling of collage fragments— resulting in a more immediate and direct solution of complex formal problems. The very passion of his approach to this contemporary apex of tragedy and the very grandeur of his conception of spiritual invincibility heightened his creative processes as never before.

The remarkable synthesis, the physical and mystical unity and the totality of form that marked the major achievements of Lebrun's last five years were anticipated to a considerable extent by the works based on the death camps and by those of the *Hostages* series which followed.

Once more Lebrun himself was best able to articulate this climactic development in his oeuvre:

Once they said I could draw as a bird sings. Possibly I still can. But there came a time when the image of man was so defaced that bird songs did not seem enough. If I had to lose all my virtues as a passable draftsman for the sake of speaking truly about the unmanageable design of our condition, I would do so gladly. Talent is one thing: life another.

But bird song indeed—and what have classical clarity and unity got to do with the dread unity of the charnel house pit? At best strangers to each

other, even in passion when alive, the dead are now one single common body.

James Thrall Soby suggests that Lebrun's preoccupation with the evidence of man's inhumanity to man once more focused his attention on the artistic ancestor closest to him—on Goya, whose eloquence stems from similar preoccupations and observations of war and carnage. Having finished the large scale works commemorative of the victims of Nazi butchery, Lebrun embarked on the creation of a series of Goyescas climaxed by such memorable works as *Familia Real* and *Portrait of a Spanish Nobleman*. As Soby remarked "...to make this sort of original and penetrating commentary on the style and iconography of a predecessor in the history of art is a very considerable achievement indeed."

In Goya Lebrun found "...all that the human cage can contain of malice, lust contradiction and splendor in the world of paint, a world of maniacs dolled up like butterflies, or the dual image to express what we all carry in us." These explorations of Goya were instrumental in further clarifying Lebrun's idiom. He was about to shift his vision. Critic Langsner observed that the artist "...now moved the viewer inside the event, doing away with the detached observer."

The final metamorphosis of Lebrun's figurative abstractions resulted in amorphous and ambiguous island forms of monumental porportions which first emerged with *Doble Disparate* in 1958 and *Standing Figures* in 1959 and found their mystical and plastic consolidation in the haunting *Night Figures* of 1962. Here Lebrun put himself into the very center of the pictorial event he was creating, completely engaged at last—unable and unwilling to step back from the work at hand to gain a more detached view. Nor did he look over his shoulders to see whether his audience was frowning or applauding.

Finally Lebrun had pushed the physical limitations of his subject matter, of his arena, and of his mind and vision so far that the resultant forms, though clearly figurative in origin, emerged as colossi that have superhuman implications. These late configurations project a sense of cosmological unity unprecedented in Lebrun's work. The interior and exterior realities of man now became interchangeable in Lebrun's transfigurations and represented the end-result of the artist's life-long exploration of the figure in terms of its terrain, its architecture and its organic imperatives.

The major works of the last six years of his life make clear that despite the agonic quality of much of his work, this central aim was not to immerse us in images of decay and defeat, but to achieve a spiritual and pictorial metamorphosis that is essentially affirmative—indeed, anti-death.

Doubtless the preparation and execution of the *Genesis* mural at Pomona College (described in Dr. Peter Selz' essay) constituted a catalytic event in the artist's life which enabled him to move farther towards an essential synthesis of intent and accomplishment, of observation and invention than he had ever been able to achieve before.

This amazing sense of unity is found to an even greater degree in the graphic equivalents to Lebrun's deepest feelings revealed in the *Night Figures* and *Twilight Figures* paintings and in the drawings and prints inspired by the literary symbolism of Dante, Melville and Brecht.

Long an admirer of Lebrun's creative powers, Daniel Catton Rich was moved to write that

"...at last draftsman and painter have fused. The chief material for his expression was the human body. No artist in America has made more splendid or expressive use of it. He loved its structure so passionately that he could bisect it, spread it out, mutilate and fragmentize it and finally—at the end—come to harmony with it in those huge looming figures which embody his last poetry...

Though Lebrun insisted on more than design, he constantly stressed more than subject. He painted not men but Man. His great themes found their expression in great form... He remained aloof from those 'frenetic' movements which constantly disturb the art world. He worked with tremendous intensity, driving himself to the last moment of desperate effort. Yet these works shine with a clarity and there is no sense of strain. In some ways he was a solitary...at the same time there is nothing lonely about his art. It reaches out to you, the spectator, with grandeur of form and passionate communication of spirit."

In my own view the most telling works in Lebrun's entire protean production are his drawings based on Dante's *Inferno*. By the time these magnificent drawings were included in a retrospective mounted by Jules Heller at USC in 1961, I had closely observed Lebrun's evolution as an artist for over a decade. It seemed to me that in recent years he had come further than ever before in his search for the monolithic semblance of form without the chatter of detail. In the dark, amorphous images created during the last six years of Lebrun's life their sense of sorrow is not born out of anger but out of empathy and pity. Their sense of anguish is softened by identification and compassion.

For Dante, Melville and Brecht, Lebrun became an illuminator rather than an illustrator. If he shared the brutality of some of their visions, it was not for the sake of brutality but out of a need to graphically project man's inexorable tragedy in a manner that, in its highest form, became exultant.

Sculpture

The prison of the studio and the easel from which Lebrun had such rare escapes through the ridiculously few mural commissions that came his way, was burst by him when he turned his attention to sculpture in 1962. This seemingly inevitable metamorphosis brought his concern with the multiplicity of shape into the three dimensional realm. A few earlier sculptural exercises were tentative and confined to relief.

In sculpture Lebrun finally found that rewarding sense of absolute physical identification with his work that he had always been seeking. The quick revisions possible in wax were even more expedient to him than his phenomenal rapidity in drawing. By his own account he felt himself working with a kind of absorption that was "like a dream". As he continued to wrest powerfully poetic shapes out of a variety of sculptural materials in the face of a rapidly waning state of health, Lebrun felt all of his perceptions and his accumulation of plastic knowledge mobilized.

The most revealing testimony about the makings of some 30 impressive sculptures in the last two years of Lebrun's life comes from George Goyer who became his assistant and who has been instrumental in the casting of all the late sculptural works.

A young artist with some sculptural experience, Goyer came under Lebrun's strong influence when that artist served as Regents Professor at the University of California at Santa Barbara where his close friends Howard Warshaw and William Ptaszynski were members of the faculty. As Lebrun's assistant in sculpture it was Goyer who obtained the necessary materials and tools for this endeavor.

With enormous devotion and piercing intelligence Goyer has been a central part in the realization of Lebrun's sculpture. This resulted in his extensive involvement with casting techniques and in his eventually becoming a partner in the San Francisco Art Foundry, where all the posthumous casts were executed under his supervision.

"Rico very quickly explored the range and possibilities of wax and, at the same time, met the demands of this engagement of form and materials with incredible freshness and invention. The waxes began to grow around us, dimensional analogies to his drawings and collages," Goyer wrote in a letter to me. Reflecting the lasting reality of their collaboration Goyer then continues in the present tense:

Rico being Rico takes anything around him which, it occurs to him, might nourish his growing piece of form with its own peculiar needs, and much occurs to him. He works with a cold deliberation. These discoveries are not made with an exclamation mark but flow through him naturally, on their way to becoming form.

One of my own last unforgettable encounters with Rico Lebrun came on the sun porch of the home of his close friends, Edith and Frank Wyle, where he had spent several periods between the hospitalizations forced by repeated episodes of surgery.

Propped in his sick bed, wan and weak, unable to rise, the pain plainly written in his face, Lebrun never seemed more obsessively creative to me as when I observed him firmly, explicitly and with occasional flashes of humor, direct Goyer while the young man struggled, welding torch in hand, to correct mistakes made on the *Soaring Figure* by a foundry confounded by the innovations of his sculptural vocabulary. It was late in January 1964. Lebrun, in the

face of immense physical suffering and knowing that his cancer was incurable, remained at work.

The Other Side of the Mirror

For many years Lebrun had dreamed of a studio-home where both his work and his family would be fully at home. Its construction coincided with the advent of his fatal illness. That artist's last, heroic struggle was to survive, if only for a few days, so that he could live and work in his new Malibu home. It was this incredible effort that was touchingly described by Howard Warshaw, as friends and family gathered in Malibu right after the artist's death on May 9, 1964. In his moving talk, Warshaw described a conversation that he had with Lebrun on the morning of New Year's Day.

"It was a vividly clear and sparkling day on lower Sixth Street, and Rico knew his fate. After a rueful smile, when I entered the room, he said: 'The game of hide-and-seek with terror is over. I am on the other side of the mirror.'

This was said, I think, partially to put me at my ease, but later I thought: what did he mean, what would he see on the other side of the mirror? And finally I think I know what he meant: he would see everything except the reflection of himself. To see the world even for a very short time with this sublime indifference could be a very beautiful period. From then on I hoped that he would have the strength of mind and body to show us his vision. For a long time it looked as though he would not, while Constance resolutely prepared his house for him...But he came home, and rose again, and put his hand once more to the page. His undiminished spirit, with almost no muscle left at his disposal, took a serene calm look at the grace of his failing flesh and made the drawings of his hand over there on the wall. This studio yielded up five drawings for us, and in spite of his pain it was a period of intense happiness for him."

So the central theme of Lebrun's life—his obsessive compulsion to work—reached to his very death. At the threshhold of death he himself acted out his unwavering belief that "...our image even when disfigured by adversity is grand in meaning."

The exigencies of space for a catalog essay make it impossible to explore fully a life and an oeuvre so complex and tumultuous as Lebrun's. There remains the need for a thorough evaluation of his enormous contribution as a teacher which not only moulded several generations of California artists but extended to the Mexican painters once grouped under the "Nueva Presencia" label and their noted contemporary Jose Luis Cuevas and, late in Lebrun's career, to such major East Coast artists as Leonard Baskin.

Nor can posterity be satisfied much longer with the compressed autobiographical fragments left by Lebrun when we need to learn so much about him and his work by a searching, detailed look at his often tortured yet also somehow highly fulfilled life. And since this exhibition is limited to drawings, paintings and sculpture, a critical discussion of his remarkable printmaking ventures must await another occasion.

Confronting the works at hand, we conclude that the repeated attempts to dismiss Lebrun as an anachronism or to obscure his forceful contributions by lumping him among the so-called "neo-humanists" cannot succeed much longer in denying him his just place as one of the foremost artists of his time.

Lebrun was a Baroque artist if we mean that he made use of his own immense contemporary inventiveness to animate the pictorial or sculptural event to the utmost. But it had nothing to do with "Baroqueness" or deadly historicism.

"The true meaning of the Baroque masters is to me not their bravura (which was the product of a deep need too) but that they dared break the 'categorical' of classicism with the new concept of multiple, animated image," Lebrun wrote to Donald Bear early in his maturity. "Our time continues them not in revival but in essence.

I must start with the tangible object, the concrete. My aim is to fashion its equivalent concreteness in paint and line. To point up this quality of existence necessitates elimination, invention and abstraction. Abstraction is the concrete revealed.

To abstract is an intensely human function. Some very fine works of abstraction have been said to lack humaneness. Yet they were performed by

humans, are human works, which is far more pertinent
than their looking like humans. On the other hand,
the baseness of certain literalisms in art is,
at times, truly inhuman."

Poet John Ciardi summed up the burning spirit of
Lebrun memorably: "The more contemplative and
detached artist can create well enough in a relatively
relaxed and philosophical way. But the splendid ones
always burn. The true passion is for the impossible.
The work of the true artist is a creative violence,
an attempt on the unattainable, and violent with the
blazing of its own intensity. The artist must rush to the
encounter with form because time is forever running out.
Rico Lebrun was such a compulsive creator.
And one driven still harder by the dark irony of time,
for certainly his powers were gathering to their
fullest just when death began to say no to his body."

From the other side of the mirror, Lebrun himself
leaves us with a question that must be answered
by succeeding generations of artists determined to
push further on the path he extended into the
nether world where form and spirit merge:

Why talk about neo-humanism? Why not decide
if man is worth featuring? Is he to be disqualified
in the field of vision?
To me the vertebrate marvel contains new
sights for the eyes. Its terrain cannot be prefabricated
by geometry, nor found through bizarre accident;
it may now and then condescend to be
measured by love.

22) SHROUD ON THE ARM OF THE CROSS, 1950   36″ x 121″

19) MACHINE GUN, 1950   11″ x 60″

24) TERESA, 1952   51$\frac{1}{2}$" x 41$\frac{1}{2}$"

Paintings

1) CARTOON FOR MURAL, 1935
Oil on canvas
16" x 72"
Channing Peake, Beverly Hills, California

2) SELF-PORTRAIT, about 1940
Oil on canvas
16" x 12"
Santa Barbara Museum of Art, California

3) BULLRING, 1943
Oil on canvas
6" x 9"
Estate of Rico Lebrun

4) CLOTH, 1945
Oil on canvas
21" x 26¼"
Santa Barbara Museum of Art, California

5) ROPE, 1945
Oil on canvas
46" x 26"
Santa Barbara Museum of Art, California

6) STILL LIFE WITH WINE FLASK, 1945
Oil on canvas
32" x 26"
Santa Barbara Museum of Art, California

7) PORTUGUESE HARROW, 1945
Oil on canvas
46½" x 58"
Santa Barbara Museum of Art, California

8) UNTITLED (WOUNDED ITALIAN SOLDIERS),
NOT DATED
Oil on canvas
20" x 30"
Howard Warshaw, Carpinteria, California

9) BLACK PLOW, 1947
Casein on masonite
79" x 36"
Mrs. Donald Bear,
Santa Barbara, California

10) WHEEL, about 1947
Oil on canvas
53" x 33"
The Honorable and Mrs. William Benton,
Southport, Connecticut

11) FARM MACHINE #1, 1947
Oil on canvas
36" x 72"
Mr. and Mrs. Michael Straight,
Washington, D.C.

12) WOOD OF THE HOLY CROSS, 1948
Oil and casein on canvas
80" x 30"
Whitney Museum of American Art,
New York

13) WOMAN OF THE CRUCIFIXION, 1948
Casein and oil on canvas
71⅞" x 41¾"
Estate of Rico Lebrun

14) WOMAN OF THE CRUCIFIXION, 1948
Oil on canvas
70" x 40"
Yale University Art Gallery, Gift of
the William C. Whitney Foundation,
New Haven, Connecticut

15) BURNT SPINNER, 1948
Oil on canvas
80" x 30"
Mr. Paul W. Zimmerman,
Hartford, Connecticut

16) THE YELLOW PLOW, 1949
Oil on upson board
80" x 36"
Munson-Williams-Proctor Institute,
Utica, New York

17) WOMAN OF THE CRUCIFIXION, 1948-1950
Duco on masonite
96" x 48"
University of Nebraska, Lincoln

18) SOLDIER ASLEEP AT THE FOOT
OF THE CROSS, 1950
Duco on masonite
48" x 35"
Willard Straight Hall, Cornell University,
on loan from Michael Straight,
Washington, D.C.

19) MACHINE GUN, 1950
Casein on canvas
11" x 60"
Collection of Mr. and Mrs. M. F. Feheley,
Toronto, Canada

20) TREAD OF TANK, 1950
Duco on upson board
38" x 96"
Lee Nordness Galleries, Inc., New York

21) ARMORED CREATURE #2, 1950
Duco on masonite
11¼" x 35½"
Mrs. Donald Bear,
Santa Barbara, California

22) SHROUD ON THE ARM OF THE CROSS, 1950
Duco on upson board
36" x 121"
The Cleveland Museum of Art, Ohio
Gift of the Artist

23) THE MAGDALENE, 1950
Tempera on board
64" x 48"
Santa Barbara Museum of Art, California

24) TERESA, 1952
Duco on masonite
51½" x 41½"
Mrs. Muriel Harris, New York

25) MEMORIAL TO CAIAZZO, 1952
Casein on board
49" x 37"
Mr. and Mrs. Leonard Titleman, New York

26) THE BARBEQUE, 1953
Duco on board
24" x 60"
Mr. and Mrs. Melvin Hirsch,
Beverly Hills, California

27) MEXICAN STREET IN THE RAIN, 1954
Collage
110" x 65"
Estate of Rico Lebrun

28) BATTLE OF SAMURAI, 1955
Oil on board
48" x 128"
Mr. and Mrs. John Rex,
Northfork, California

29) STUDY FROM MEXICO, 1955
Oil on canvas
76" x 29"
Collection of the Silvan Simone Gallery,
Los Angeles, California

30) STUDY FROM THE "TRIUMPH OF DEATH"
BY TRAINI, 1955-1956
Oil and ink on paper
58¼" x 93½"
Los Angeles County Museum of Art,
California
Anonymous Loan

31) STUDY FOR BUCHENWALD CART, 1956
Oil on board
48" x 72"
Selden Rodman,
Oakland, New Jersey

32) THE LISTENING DEAD, 1957
Oil on upson board
96" x 48"
The Pennsylvania Academy of
The Fine Arts, Philadelphia

33) MARIA LUISA, 1958
Oil on upson board
79¹/₂" x 40"
Estate of Rico Lebrun

34) DOBLE DISPARATE, 1958
Oil and casein on plywood
84" x 45¹/₂"
Extended loan to the Museum
of Modern Art, New York,
from Mr. and Mrs. Frank S. Wyle

35) FLOOR OF BUCHENWALD #2, 1958
Casein and ink on board
48" x 96"
Mr. and Mrs. Leslie L. Johnson,
Dayton, Ohio

36) PORTRAIT OF SPANISH NOBLEMAN
AFTER GOYA, 1958
Oil on canvas
57" x 46"
Selden Rodman, Oakland, New Jersey

37) BIG SITTING WOMAN, 1959
Watercolor
40¹/₂" x 26¹/₂"
Mr. and Mrs. Sidney S. Kingsley, New York

38) NIGHT FIGURES #2, 1961
Oil on canvas
78³/₄" x 108⁵/₈"
Gift of the Friends of the Corcoran Gallery
Corcoran Gallery of Art, Washington, D.C.

39) FLOATING FIGURE, 1961
Casein and oil on canvas
98" x 48"
Lee Nordness Galleries, Inc., New York

40) FIGURE IN THE FLOOD, 1962
Casein on board
96" x 48"
Art-U.S.A., The Johnson Collection,
Racine, Wisconsin

41) SPLIT FIGURE FROM DANTE'S INFERNO, 1962
Casein on board
34" x 48"
Lee Nordness Galleries, Inc., New York

42) NIGHT FIGURES #1, 1962
Oil on canvas
92" x 74"
Lee Nordness Galleries, Inc., New York

43) WRAPPED FORMS, 1963
Watercolor
28" x 40"
Lee Nordness Galleries, Inc., New York

44) RECLINING FIGURE, 1963
Oil on board
9" x 14"
Mr. and Mrs. Frank S. Wyle,
Los Angeles, California

45) CRUCIFIXION, 1963
Oil on canvas
93" x 82"
Lee Nordness Galleries, Inc., New York

Drawings

46) SELF-PORTRAIT, about 1927
Pencil and watercolor
10¹/₂" x 9"
Mrs. Morris D. Behrend, New York

47) BOOTBLACK AND STREET SWEEPER,
1927-1929
Charcoal
18" x 12³/₄"
Mrs. Morris D. Behrend, New York

48) COWLED WOMAN WITH BASKET, 1927-1929
Ink wash
19" x 13"
Mrs. Morris D. Behrend, New York

49) DON QUIXOTE, 1927-1929
Ink wash
5³/₄" x 9"
Mrs. Morris D. Behrend, New York

50) PUNCHINELLO, 1927-1929
Ink wash
10¹/₄" x 7³/₄"
Mrs. Morris D. Behrend, New York

51) TWO CLOWNS, 1927-1929
Ink wash
13³/₄" x 10³/₄"
Mrs. Morris D. Behrend, New York

52) ANNA, about 1931
Chalk and crayon
72" x 36"
Santa Barbara Museum of Art, California

53) CROUCHING GIRL, 1932
Conte crayon
29¹/₂" x 21¹/₂"
Fogg Art Museum, Harvard University,
Cambridge, Massachusetts
Gift of Rico Lebrun

54) RECLINING OX, 1932
Charcoal
10 3/4" x 15 3/5"
Miss Agnes Mongan,
Cambridge, Massachusetts

55) CARTOON FOR MINERS MURAL, 1934
Charcoal and sepia
80" x 42"
Mr. and Mrs. Michael Straight,
Washington, D.C.

56) WOMAN WITH LANTERN
(CARTOON FROM FLOOD), about 1936
Charcoal and sepia
72" x 34"
Mr. and Mrs. Norton Simon,
Los Angeles, California

57) FIGURE IN DUST STORM, 1936
Ink and chalk
24¹/₂" x 18"
Santa Barbara Museum of Art, California

58) SLAUGHTER HOUSE, 1937
Ink
7" x 11"
Mr. and Mrs. Norton Simon,
Los Angeles, California

59) THE DYING HORSE, 1939
Ink and chalk
19" x 25"
Mrs. Donald B. Ayres, Jr.,
Newport Beach, California

60) IL MALOCCHIO, about 1940
Ink
21" x 29"
Mr. and Mrs. Norton Simon,
Los Angeles, California

61) THE HOLY GHOST, 1940
Ink
14" x 10"
Mr. and Mrs. Norton Simon,
Los Angeles, California

62) GOD MADE ADAM OUT OF MUD,
about 1940
Ink wash
16³/₄" x 11¹/₂"
The North Carolina Museum of Art,
Raleigh

63) MUSICIAN, 1940
Ink
28" x 20"
Museum of Modern Art, New York,
purchase

64) PORTRAIT OF KATE LAWSON, 1940
Ink and chalk
40" x 36"
Collection of Mr. and Mrs. M. F. Feheley,
Toronto, Canada

65) SEATED CLOWN, 1941
Ink, chalk and sanguine
39¹/₂" x 29"
Santa Barbara Museum of Art, California

66) ROLLING STEER, 1941
Ink and chalk
19" x 25¹/₂"
Fogg Art Museum, Harvard University,
Cambridge, Massachusetts
Gift of Arthur Sachs

67) EROICA, 1941
Ink and chalk
33¹/₂" x 25¹/₂"
Mrs. Guenn Farrington,
Santa Barbara, California

68) WOMAN LEANING ON A STAFF, 1941
Ink and chalk
25¹/₄" x 11¹/₄"
Thomas A. Freiberg,
Los Angeles, California

69) STUDY FROM GOYA, 1941
Ink and pencil
25" x 19"
Mr. and Mrs. Leslie L. Johnson,
Dayton, Ohio

70) ORTENSIA SEATED, 1941
Pencil
25¹/₂" x 20"
Mrs. Donald Bear,
Santa Barbara, California

71) NIGHT, 1942
Pencil
19" x 25"
Mrs. Donald Bear,
Santa Barbara, California

72) CICADA, 1942
Ink
28" x 36"
Mr. and Mrs. Robert J. Levyn,
Los Angeles, California

73) WAR STUDY, 1942
Ink
19¹/₂" x 21¹/₂"
Mr. and Mrs. Norton Simon,
Los Angeles, California

74) STUDY OF SQUIRREL, 1945
Ink and chalk
17¹/₂" x 12¹/₂"
Santa Barbara Museum of Art,
California

75) FLORA, 1945
Ink
19" x 25"
Mr. and Mrs. Norton Simon,
Los Angeles, California

76) CRIPPLE WITH BIRDCAGE, 1945
Ink
25" x 19"
Los Angeles County Museum of Art,
California

77) THE MASSACRE OF THE INNOCENTS, 1948
Ink
10" x 15"
Mr. and Mrs. Ross R. DeVean,
Riverside, California

78) PLANT (THISTLE), 1946
Ink
23¹/₄" x 29"
Santa Barbara Museum of Art, California

79) SUNFLOWER, 1947
Ink
19" x 25"
Dr. and Mrs. Albert S. Chase,
Los Angeles, California

80) STRAVINSKY, 1947
Charcoal
20" x 17"
Selden Rodman, Oakland, New Jersey

81) FLEEING MOTHER AND CHILD, 1948
Ink
19" x 24"
Mr. and Mrs. Mayer Greenberg,
Los Angeles, California

82) FLIGHT, about 1948
Ink and chalk
19" x 25"
Mr. and Mrs. Norton Simon,
Los Angeles, California

83) RUNNING WOMAN WITH CHILD, 1948
Ink
18³/₄" x 25³/₈"
University of Nebraska,
Lincoln

84) STRUMMING TROUBADOUR, 1948
Ink
15" x 9"
Mr. and Mrs. James A. Wood,
Riverside, California

85) SEATED WOMAN #2, 1948
Ink
25" x 19"
Mr. and Mrs. Leslie L. Johnson,
Dayton, Ohio

86) COSTUME FOR BALLET BY
CARMELITA MARACCI, 1948
Ink and crayon
25" x 19¹/₂"
Mr. and Mrs. Leslie L. Johnson,
Dayton, Ohio

87) TURTLE SOLDIER, 1949
Ink on illustration board
19¹/₂" x 29¹/₂"
Metropolitan Museum of Art,
Rogers Fund, 1955, New York

88) SKETCH FOR CRUCIFIXION #6, 1949
Ink wash
20" x 26"
Mr. and Mrs. Winslow Ames,
Saunderstown, Rhode Island

89) WOMAN OF THE CRUCIFIXION, 1948
Chalk and ink
24" x 19"
Mrs. Constance Lebrun Crown,
Malibu, California

90) UNTITLED (HEADLESS FEMALE NUDE), 1948
Ink
24$^{1}/_{2}$" x 16"
Mr. and Mrs. James Pinto,
San Miguel de Allende, Mexico

91) FRAGMENT OF THE CRUCIFIXION, 1949
Ink wash
7" x 17$^{3}/_{4}$"
Mr. and Mrs. Leslie L. Johnson,
Dayton, Ohio

92) ARMORED PLANT, 1949
Ink
22" x 31"
Dr. and Mrs. Milton Gardiner,
Merrick, New York

93) SKETCH FOR CRUCIFIXION, 1950
Ink wash
15" x 40"
Mrs. Constance Lebrun Crown,
Malibu, California

94) MAGDALENE, 1950
Ink and pencil
38$^{1}/_{2}$" x 30"
Collection of Mr. and Mrs. M. F. Feheley,
Toronto, Canada

95) SCENE FROM CRUCIFIXION, about 1950
Ink wash on bristol board
14" x 27$^{1}/_{2}$"
Mrs. Constance Lebrun Crown,
Malibu, California

96) CRUCIFIXION SCENE, 1950
Ink wash
25" x 19"
Mr. and Mrs. Leslie L. Johnson,
Dayton, Ohio

97) SKETCH FOR CRUCIFIXION, 1950
Ink and wash on bristol board
13$^{1}/_{4}$" x 27$^{1}/_{2}$"
The North Carolina Museum of Art,
Raleigh

98) WOMAN OF THE CRUCIFIXION, 1950
Ink and chalk
14" x 9"
Channing Peake, Beverly Hills, California

99) SAINT CHRISTOPHER, 1950
Ink
15$^{1}/_{2}$" x 12"
Mrs. Otto L. Spaeth, New York

100) CARPENTER OF THE CROSS, 1950
Charcoal
60" x 40"
Collection of the Silvan Simone Gallery,
Los Angeles, California

101) SCENE OF CRUCIFIXION, 1950
Ink
14" x 27$^{1}/_{2}$"
Mr. and Mrs. David Thorne,
Pasadena, California

102) UNTITLED, 1950
Charcoal and ink
40" x 30"
Howard Warshaw, Carpinteria, California

103) MARY AT THE CROSS, 1951
Ink wash
23" x 28$^{1}/_{2}$"
Mr. and Mrs. Sidney Deutsch,
White Plains, New York

104) UNTITLED (SEATED MAN), 1951
Ink
19" x 20$^{1}/_{2}$"
Mr. and Mrs. James Pinto,
San Miguel de Allende, Mexico

105) SINDACATO, 1951
Ink
25" x 18$^{1}/_{2}$"
Mr. and Mrs. James Pinto,
San Miguel de Allende, Mexico

106) DRAWING FOR A POEM BY AUDEN, 1951
Ink and chalk
30" x 24"
Mr. and Mrs. Stuart E. Weaver, Jr.,
Los Angeles, California

107) FIESTA, 1952
Ink
19" x 25"
Dr. and Mrs. Mac L. Sherwood,
Beverly Hills, California

108) UNTITLED (WOMAN AND HORSE),
1953 or 1954
Ink
18$^{1}/_{2}$" x 23$^{3}/_{4}$"
Dr. Francisco Olsina,
San Miguel de Allende, Mexico

109) UNTITLED (SINVERGUENZAS),
1953 or 1954
Ink
23$^{3}/_{4}$" x 18$^{1}/_{2}$"
Dr. Francisco Olsina,
San Miguel de Allende, Mexico

110) UNTITLED (DANCER AND BULL),
1953 or 1954
Ink
18$^{1}/_{4}$" x 23$^{1}/_{2}$"
Dr. Francisco Olsina,
San Miguel de Allende, Mexico

111) ARMORED SLAB, LACE TEARS —
GOLGOTHA WALL, 1954
Ink wash
79" x 87$^{1}/_{2}$"
Estate of Rico Lebrun

112) PORTRAIT OF HOWARD WARSHAW, 1956
Collage, gesso, ink wash and tempera
61" x 41"
Estate of Rico Lebrun

113) STUDY FROM ORCAGNA, 1957
Ink
24$^{1}/_{8}$" x 18$^{3}/_{4}$"
Mr. and Mrs. Leslie L. Johnson,
Dayton, Ohio

114) SAMURAI, 1957
Ink wash
23" x 18"
Mr. and Mrs. Frank S. Wyle,
Los Angeles, California

115) RUNNING SAMURAI, 1957
Ink wash
36" x 24"
Mr. and Mrs. Frank S. Wyle,
Los Angeles, California

116) MULE AND GOAT (GOYESCA), 1957
Ink wash
30" x 19"
Mr. and Mrs. Sumner Gerstein,
Brookline, Massachusetts

117) STUDY FROM GOYA, 1957
Ink and pencil
31$^{1}/_{2}$" x 25"
Mr. and Mrs. Leslie L. Johnson,
Dayton, Ohio

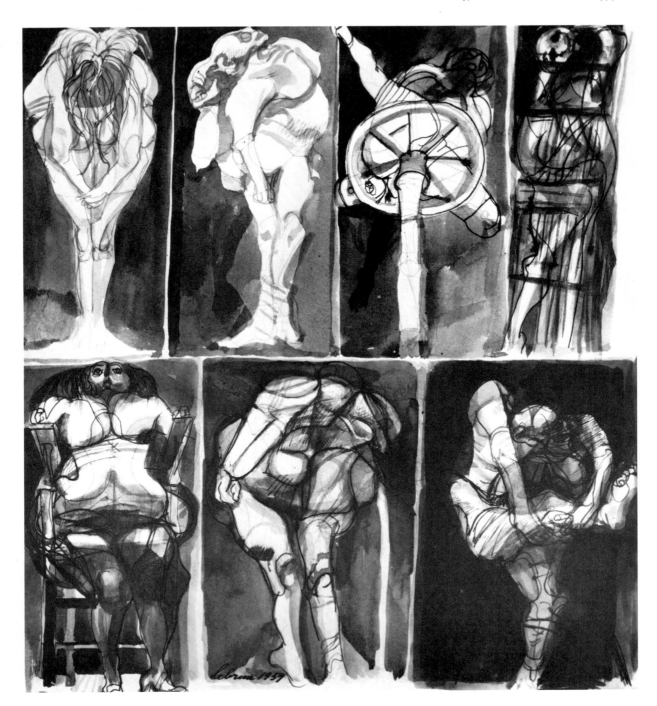

lebrun 1959

118) UNTITLED (FIGURES), 1958
Ink and pastel
19¹/₂" x 25¹/₂"
Dr. Francisco Olsina,
San Miguel de Allende, Mexico

119) MEMBERS OF THE RESURRECTION, 1958
Ink wash and wax
28¹/₂" x 22¹/₂"
Robert W. Service, Burbank, California

120) UNTITLED (NOSOTROS-PACO RICO), 1958
Ink and gouache
25" x 19¹/₄"
Dr. Francisco Olsina,
San Miguel de Allende, Mexico

121) SITTING NUDE, 1958
Charcoal and ink
24³/₄" x 19"
Selden Rodman, Oakland, New Jersey

122) LISTENING DEAD, 1958
Casein and ink on paper
25¹/₂" x 19¹/₂"
Mr. and Mrs. William Ptaszynski,
Goleta, California

123) FAMILIA REAL, 1958
Ink on board
60" x 45"
Mr. and Mrs. Joel Grey, New York

124) PORTRAIT OF TERESA, 1958
Charcoal on canvas
72" x 54"
Estate of Rico Lebrun

125) ANNA MAGNANI IN
"THE ROSE TATOO", 1958
Ink wash
25" x 19"
Mr. and Mrs. Leslie L. Johnson,
Dayton, Ohio

126) THE CRIPPLE, 1958
Ink
28¹/₂" x 22"
Lee Nordness Galleries, Inc., New York

127) STUDY FROM GOYA'S PORTRAIT OF
MARIA LUISA, 1958
Ink and watercolor
25" x 19"
Worcester Art Museum, Massachusetts

128) CRUCIFIXION, about 1958 or 1959
Ink wash and pastel
13" x 18"
Mrs. Constance Lebrun Crown,
Malibu, California

129) PAGE FOR LOTTERY BOOK, 1959
Ink wash
23" x 20"
Mr. and Mrs. Albert Millman,
South Orange, New Jersey

130) STANDING FIGURE, 1959
Ink wash and wax
29" x 16¹/₂"
Nathaniel Saltonstall,
Boston, Massachusetts

131) GROUP FOR FLOOD, 1959
Ink wash
19³/₄" x 27¹/₄"
Miss Shelley Wexler, New York

132) FIGURE WITH BANDAGED LEGS, 1959
Ink wash and wax
30" x 15³/₄"
Miss Adele Clement, New York

133) GALAPAGOS, 1959
Ink wash
24" x 19"
Mr. and Mrs. Frank S. Wyle,
Los Angeles, California

134) TWO STANDING FIGURES, 1959
Ink wash and wax
40" x 30"
Collection of Mr. and Mrs. M. F. Feheley,
Toronto, Canada

135) FIGURES IN THE SKY, 1959
Ink
29³/₄" x 21³/₄"
Delphic Arts, New York

136) SEATED FIGURE #10, 1960
Ink
38" x 30"
Mr. and Mrs. Robert J. Levyn,
Los Angeles, California

137) NOAH, 1960
Ink wash
40" x 30"
Dr. and Mrs. Leo Rangell,
Los Angeles, California

138) TURTLE, 1960
Ink
22" x 30"
Mr. and Mrs. Robert Eichholz,
Washington, D.C.

139) FORESHORTENED MODEL, 1960
Ink wash
25" x 19"
Lee Nordness Galleries, Inc., New York

140) HEAD OF ABEL, 1960
Ink wash
30" x 22"
Mr. and Mrs. Jack Elliott,
Studio City, California

141) SEATED WOMAN, 1960
Ink wash
30" x 22"
Mr. and Mrs. Harry A. Altman,
Los Angeles, California

142) FIGHTING DEMONS, 1960
Ink wash
21¹/₂" x 29¹/₂"
Mr. and Mrs. Robert Eichholz,
Washington, D.C.

143) TORMENTED SHADES, 1961
Ink
22¹/₂" x 24"
Mrs. Constance Lebrun Crown,
Malibu, California

144) SHADES IMBEDDED IN FROZEN LAKE, 1961
Pencil
22" x 30"
Dr. and Mrs. Milton M. Gardiner,
Merrick, New York

145) GENESIS FIGURE, 1960
Ink wash
35" x 22"
Mr. and Mrs. Frank S. Wyle,
Los Angeles, California

146) FEWCOMBIE THE CRIPPLE, 1961
Ink wash
39¹/₂" x 27¹/₄"
Professor and Mrs. Edwin H. Miller,
Riverdale, New York

147) THE PEACH WITH THE WEIGHT
OF THE BEGGAR ON HER BACK, 1961
Ink wash
27" x 20¹/₂"
Lee Nordness Galleries, Inc., New York

148) BEGGARS FIGHTING LIKE
WILD BEASTS, 1961
Ink
40″ x 27″
Lee Nordness Galleries, Inc., New York

149) STUDY FOR INFERNO, 1961
Ink wash
22$^{1}/_{8}$″ x 30$^{1}/_{4}$″
Lee Nordness Galleries, Inc., New York

150) TWO BEHEADED SHADES HOLDING
OUT HEAD, 1961
Ink wash
22″ x 30″
Lee Nordness Galleries, Inc., New York

151) BEGGARS INTO FIGHTING DOGS, 1961
Ink
20″ x 28″
Lee Nordness Galleries, Inc., New York

152) HATER OF SELF, 1961
Ink
39″ x 72″
Selden Rodman, Oakland, New Jersey

153) THE SUICIDE, 1961
Ink
39″ x 27″
Selden Rodman, Oakland, New Jersey

154) INFERNO-BOLGIA DEI SERPI, 1961
Ink
18$^{1}/_{2}$″ x 24$^{1}/_{2}$″
Mr. and Mrs. Seymour Rubin,
Washington, D.C.

155) TWO HORSES, 1961
Ink and wash
22″ x 16″
Howard Warshaw, Carpinteria, California

156) HEADLESS FIGURE, 1961
Ink wash
30″ x 40″
Mr. and Mrs. Frank S. Wyle,
Los Angeles, California

157) THAIS, 1961
Ink wash
40″ x 30″
Mr. and Mrs. Frank S. Wyle,
Los Angeles, California

158) TWO MUTILATED FIGURES, 1961
Ink wash
30″ x 40″
Mr. and Mrs. Frank S. Wyle,
Los Angeles, California

159) CIRCLE OF SOULS TORMENTED
BY THE ITCH, 1961
Ink and wash
27$^{3}/_{4}$″ x 40″
Dr. and Mrs. Herman Weiner,
Beverly Hills, California

160) LONE GREAT MUTILATED FIGURE, 1961
Ink wash
39$^{3}/_{4}$″ x 28″
The Worcester Art Museum,
Massachusetts

161) CANTOS XIII:
BLEEDING-SPEAKING FIGURES, 1961
Ink wash
27$^{1}/_{2}$″ x 38$^{1}/_{2}$″
Dr. and Mrs. S. Lifschutz,
New Brunswick, New Jersey

162) FIGURES RUNNING THE GAUNTLET
OF WOUNDS, 1961
Ink wash
27$^{3}/_{4}$″ x 40″
Lee Nordness Galleries, Inc., New York

163) SEVERAL FLAMING FIGURES, 1961
Ink wash
40″ x 27$^{3}/_{4}$″
Lee Nordness Galleries, Inc., New York

164) AMMAL, about 1962
Ink wash
25$^{1}/_{2}$″ x 18$^{1}/_{2}$″
Lee Nordness Galleries, Inc., New York

165) TWO SEATED FIGURES, 1962
Ink wash
27$^{1}/_{2}$″ x 40″
Mr. and Mrs. William Ptaszynski,
Goleta, California

166) POLLY HUMILIATED BY POLLY, 1962
Ink wash
39″ x 27″
Lee Nordness Galleries, Inc., New York

167) BOLGIA OF THE THIEVES, 1962
Ink
22″ x 29″
Mr. and Mrs. Norton Simon,
Los Angeles, California

168) INTERIOR CRUCIFIXION, 1962
Ink wash
27″ x 40″
Collection of the Silvan Simone Gallery,
Los Angeles, California

169) FLOOD FIGURES, 1962
Ink wash
23″ x 29″
Mr. and Mrs. Nick B. Williams,
La Canada, California

170) HEAD OF SUPERSTITI, 1962
Ink wash
17″ x 28″
Mr. and Mrs. Bernard L. Warner,
Los Angeles, California

171) INTERIOR WITH FIGURE, 1962
Ink wash
27″ x 21″
Mr. and Mrs. Nick B. Williams,
La Canada, California

172) UNTITLED
Ink wash and wax
27$^{1}/_{2}$″ x 25$^{1}/_{2}$″
Mrs. Constance Lebrun Crown,
Malibu, California

173) KNEELING AND STANDING FIGURES, 1962
Ink wash
27$^{1}/_{2}$″ x 39$^{1}/_{2}$″
Philadelphia Museum of Art, Pennsylvania

174) WHITE BODY, 1962
Ink wash
38$^{1}/_{2}$″ x 27″
Mr. and Mrs. Mayer Greenberg,
Los Angeles, California

175) CRUCIFIXION, 1963
Mixed media on masonite
10″ x 18″
Lee Nordness Galleries, Inc., New York

176) SHELF WITH OBJECTS FROM FLOOD, 1963
Ink, wax and gouache
19″ x 27″
Mr. and Mrs. David Lebrun,
Malibu, California

177) TWO LINKED FIGURES, 1963
Ink and wax
27$^{1}/_{2}$″ x 40$^{1}/_{2}$″
Mr. and Mrs. Bernard Warner,
Los Angeles, California

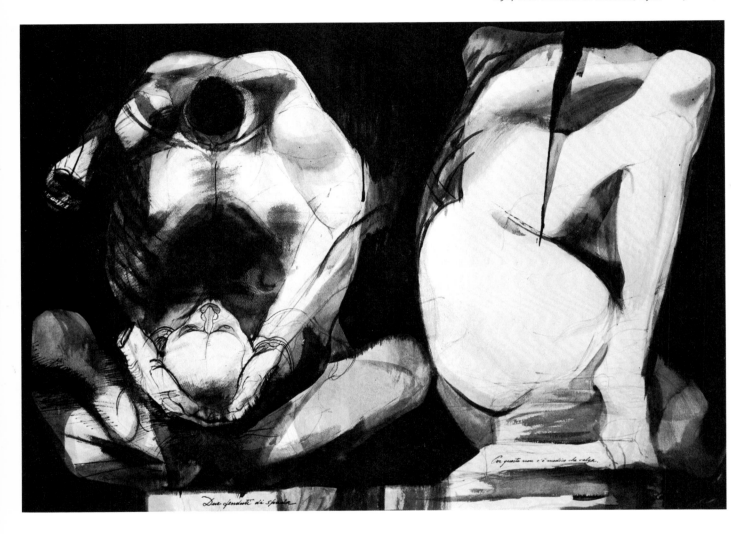

178) TWO FIGURES FOR SCULPTURE,
about 1963
Ink wash
about 60″ x 96″
Mrs. Constance Lebrun Crown,
Malibu, California

179) TWO FIGURES FOR SCULPTURE,
about 1963
Ink wash
60″ x 106″
Estate of Rico Lebrun

180) THREE HANDS, 1964
Ink
20″ x 27^1/$_2$″
Mr. and Mrs. David Lebrun,
Malibu, California

Sculpture, 1962-1963

181) FEMALE FIGURE
Stainless steel
8″ x 1^1/$_2$″
Dr. and Mrs. Albert S. Chase,
Los Angeles, California

182) STANDING FEMALE
Bronze relief
17″ x 13″
Dr. and Mrs. Albert S. Chase,
Los Angeles, California

183) SOLDIER AND WOMAN
Bronze relief
14″ x 26″
Dr. and Mrs. Sylvan Schireson,
Los Angeles, California

184) STUDY FOR JOB
Bronze relief
13″ x 12″
Mr. and Mrs. Frank S. Wyle,
Los Angeles, California

185) SOLDIER
Stainless steel
8″ x 1^1/$_2$″
Estate of Rico Lebrun

186) MINOTAUR
Bronze
16^1/$_2$″ x 5″
Estate of Rico Lebrun

187) BOUND FIGURE
Bronze
7^1/$_2$″ x 11″
Estate of Rico Lebrun

188) BIRD-HEADED FIGURE
Bronze
20″ x 7^1/$_2$″
Estate of Rico Lebrun

189) HOSED FIGURE
Bronze
20″ x 4″
Estate of Rico Lebrun

190) HAND
Bronze
8^1/$_2$″ x 5^3/$_4$″
Estate of Rico Lebrun

191) STANDING MAN
Bronze
15^1/$_2$″ x 6″
Estate of Rico Lebrun

192) MEMORIAL TO CAIAZZO
Bronze
22″ x 10″
Estate of Rico Lebrun

193) DROWNED HEAD
Bronze
9″ x 9″
Estate of Rico Lebrun

194) FOUR-SIDED NUDE
Bronze
17^1/$_2$″ x 11″
Estate of Rico Lebrun

195) SOARING FIGURE
Bronze
36″ x 36″
Estate of Rico Lebrun

196) WOMAN WITH ARMS UNDER BREAST
Bronze
18″ x 6″
Estate of Rico Lebrun

197) WOMAN WITH ARMS OVER HEAD
Bronze
29^1/$_2$″ x 9″
Estate of Rico Lebrun

198) TIPTOE FIGURE
Bronze
50″ x 15^1/$_2$″
Estate of Rico Lebrun

199) FRAGMENTED FIGURE
Bronze relief
11^1/$_2$″ x 22^1/$_4$″
Estate of Rico Lebrun

200) FLOOD FIGURES
Bronze
16″ x 18^1/$_2$″
Estate of Rico Lebrun

201) QUILTED LEG FIGURE
Bronze
7″ x 3″
Estate of Rico Lebrun

202) RECLINING FEMALE
Bronze
10^1/$_2$″ x 3^3/$_4$″
Estate of Rico Lebrun

203) FOOT
Bronze
12″ x 4″
Estate of Rico Lebrun

204) MASK
Bronze
13^1/$_2$″ x 11^1/$_2$″
Estate of Rico Lebrun

205) BEARDED HEAD
Bronze
8^1/$_2$″ x 6″
Estate of Rico Lebrun

206) STANDING TORSO
Bronze
29″ x 14″
Estate of Rico Lebrun

207) LAZARUS
Bronze
38″ x 13″ with base
Estate of Rico Lebrun

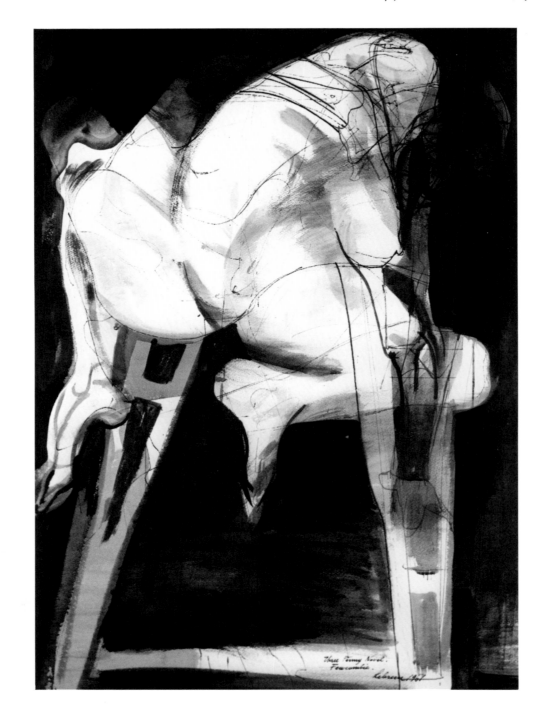

Notes on Genesis
by Peter Selz

Rico Lebrun has written of himself that he "... took to the Baroque notion long before I saw it in the museums ... Whenever I have abandoned the kinship with its essence, I have produced aesthetic exercises. Whenever I have tapped it at the core, I have felt real."[1] Lebrun's *Genesis* mural at Pomona College, notwithstanding the contemporaneity of its concept, belongs to the Baroque tradition. His drawings, growing increasingly architectural in form, his paintings, his large collages demanded the large surface of a wall. Lebrun had only once actually worked on a wall — when the Treasury Department commissioned him to do a fresco in the New York Post Office Annex (now destroyed). Twenty years later, in the autumn of 1956, during a modest one-man show of his work at the Pomona College Gallery, Lebrun visited Claremont. At Frary Hall he again admired the monumental fresco by Orozco, but at the same time he was very much impressed by the generously proportioned building itself and expressed a great desire to paint a mural in close proximity to Orozco's *Prometheus*. As chairman of the art department at Pomona, I decided to pursue this proposal: how unprecedented, but how splendid to have two great murals in a single building in America! From the beginning I was supported by James Grant and Fred Hammersley, the two painters on the College faculty, both of whom had once been Lebrun's students. Later in the fall I met Donald and Elizabeth Winston of Los Angeles who agreed with great generosity to sponsor the mural and donate it to Pomona College. There ensued an unusually fruitful collaboration between Lebrun, the Winstons, and myself.

The Board of Trustees of Pomona College expressed interest in the mural proposal but wanted to see sketches before giving final approval. Both Lebrun and myself, however, took it as a matter of artistic — and indeed academic—freedom, that an artist of established stature should not be asked to submit work to a lay committee for approval, but rather should be judged by the record of his previous achievement. In this attitude we were fully supported by the Winstons, and after some debate the College administration agreed to permit Lebrun to proceed with no restrictions whatsoever.

During the spring of 1958 Rico made repeated visits to Frary Hall and planned to prepare sketches during the academic year 1958-59 when he was to teach at Yale University. But his exuberant spirit was thoroughly depressed in New Haven by the dogmatic, Germanic attitude which then prevailed at the Yale Art School. The following year, however, when he was Artist-in-Residence at the American Academy in Rome, he devoted most of his time to sketches and finally to preliminary cartoons. He occupied a large studio at the Academy and in addition to hundreds of preparatory drawings and detailed studies, he executed cartoons ten feet in height and proportioned to the scale of the Frary wall. The iconographic theme at this time still included texts from Revelations as well as Genesis, but the basic architectural problems were solved by April 1960, when he sent a progress report to Dr. E. Wilson Lyon, President of Pomona College.

While Lebrun was in Rome the Frary wall was prepared: workmen erected a "curtain" wall designed to prevent damage to the surface from moisture and earthquake; the curtain was built and fastened to the original concrete wall by metal channels, over which was mounted a screen of steel mesh. In the summer of 1960 the artist arrived at Pomona and was joined by two assistants, James Pinto and William Ptaszynski. Pinto had previously worked in Mexico on a number of murals and Ptaszynski was a student and close friend of Lebrun.

During the working process Lebrun made numerous revisions. "The traditional procedure of completing a design, then enlarging, tracing and painting was not followed by Rico at Pomona."[2] Instead, he made constant alterations, assembling and disassembling cartoons and using the collage technique with which he had become familiar several years earlier while working in Mexico. It is interesting to recall that when I mentioned to him years earlier that I felt a lack of completion in his Mexican collages, Lebrun replied that he thought of them only as preliminary sketches for some future project. During the summer of 1960 "the collage was temporarily hung to the wall in sections with masking tape—and then was subjected to prolonged and extensive shifting, filling in, eliminations, enlargements or reductions of figure sizes, mock ups of toned papers,

drawing and re-drawing in various media, and trial changes of figure identities..."[3] In other words, the working process itself suggested changes and, although the basic design of the wall had been predetermined, both forms and images were altered.[4] The passages from the Book of Revelations were eventually abandoned, the figures of Jeremiah and Job originally on the right side of the wall disappeared to make room for Cain and Abel, while Jeremiah vanished entirely and Job, transformed in shape and content, was moved into the upper right lunette. One might almost say that action painting was carried to the wall itself by Rico Lebrun at Pomona, but perhaps this is how Tintoretto too proceeded at San Rocco.

Lebrun's medium was vinyl acetate, produced by dissolving clear vinyl pellets in acetone diluted with anhydrous alcohol. Lebrun used this medium in a highly diluted solution so that it had the consistency of an ink wash. Only black and brown pigments were used. The white of the mural is the white gesso of the curtain wall itself. The color was applied in layers of thin washes, resulting in a general transparent effect almost resembling watercolor. Light streams in directly through the arches below the mural and the sensation of color varies with the time of day: in the early morning it may have an icy, bluish cast, while at noon, with the red tile of the floor reflected on the wall, it may have a light rose tint. The only colors surrounding the mural are whitewashed walls and the gray travertine of columns and arches. The areas directly below the mural on either side are painted in solid black "in order to discourage the inevitable temptation of sgraffity."[5]

In December 1960 Rico Lebrun signed the wall, having completed a feat which in sheer size compares with Michelangelo's fresco over the altar of the Sistine Chapel (Genesis is 29 feet high, the Last Judgment measures 33 feet in height). The Pomona mural was officially dedicated on February 26, 1961.

The Genesis mural is not visible from the exterior courtyard. It is on the interior wall of Frary Hall, and has been designed to be visible from three distinct viewpoints: directly below from the steps, from the loggia floor (this is the main vantage point), and from an elevated balcony facing the mural wall.

"All the figures have this multi-viewpoint," Lebrun said. "A single viewpoint on any figure wouldn't go. The figures are deployed like opening a clam... The figures all have a barrel-like shape to repeat the tremendous curved shape of the arches. If I didn't do this, they would look too small, like a pebble in a great box or like whistling a song instead of orchestrating it."[6]

The ribs of the loggia ceiling were repeated by Lebrun in the center of the mural as the ribs of Noah's Ark, and at only one point, in the lunette of Sodom and Gomorrah on the upper right, does he permit his figures to spill out of the severe architectural framework. Scale was, of course, of primary importance. While Lebrun did not wish his figures to "rattle like pebbles in a great box," he also did not wish to overwhelm or diminish the viewer.[7] His purpose was clearly to induce in the viewer the experience of increased stature. Moreover, the use of the nude human figure directly communicates a life-enhancing and invigorating sensation of vitality. This quality of the nude has been exploited since the sculpture of the Egyptians and Greeks and articulated by thinkers on art from Goethe to Berenson. A sense of tragedy prevails in the mural, as it does in so much of Lebrun's work, yet never assumes the character of despair: " The human image, even when disfigured by the executioner, is grand in meaning."[8]

Confronting the mural, the viewer identifies with the entwined figures of Adam and Eve who, turning their backs to the spectator, witness the drama unfolding on the wall. Instead of emerging from Adam's rib, Lebrun's Eve is intrinsically bound to Adam in a welding together of forms. But if Adam and Eve are still separate entities, Cain and Abel above them are molded into a single figure, a large, heavy, powerful hulk. By merging them into one, Lebrun comments on their partnership in guilt and the identification of the killer with the killed. Abel has indeed become his brother's keeper.

The group of ravaged, pig-like people in the upper right refers to Sodom and Gomorrah, but these carcasses are not actually closely related to the story of Lot. They are derived, rather, from Lebrun's preoccupation with the funnel-like pits of Dachau and

Buchenwald, and resemble his drawings and paintings of the death camps. Here too "pain has a geometry of its own"[9] — bodies are spread like the spokes of a wheel with the cluster of heads converging below the lunette. As he often did, Lebrun here too operates in the realm between abstraction and realism, between geometry and life. But, not wishing to be frozen by the symmetry of the wall, he permitted his figures to spill, breaking through the architectural demarcation of the lunette.

Contained in the opposite lunette is the anguished figure of Job, the only character in the mural whose origin is not in the Book of Genesis. Originally this lunette was occupied by the Apocalyptic Beast. When the artist decided on Job he was for some time under the spell of the resigned and smitten Job in William Blake's visionary engravings. Blake's Job then merged with Lebrun's memories of his own earlier drawings of Neapolitan beggars on crutches. And finally the image of the Hiroshima man emerged. This Job then is no longer the submissive man of sorrow, but a victim who protests his suffering, who calls out: "I cry out of wrong, but I am not heard: I cry aloud, but there is no judgement."[10]

While in Mexico Lebrun witnessed the devastation caused by a great flood of the Santa Ynez river. He was struck by the power of the river, the twisted trees, the scooped-out roots, and hooked oak trees —by nature's mass transformed through energy forces. And the whole left side of the mural below the lunette is given over to the victims of the Deluge. They too are in a state of metamorphosis and transformation. These interlocked figures seem to struggle and carry each other; they clamber over one another to reach the protection of the Ark, only to find that the Ark is practically destroyed and no safety exists.

Lebrun "referred to Noah as a tower, a rock under cascades of surf . . . He also called Noah a fortress, a shelter, a protective paternal figure."[11] This magnificent form is clothed in a great shroud, a cloak which has become a fortress. He is the image of hope and human strength. His bowed head, derived from drawings of seaweed and yucca plants, is the central image on the wall. The timbers of the Ark surround and embrace this monumental figure and are repeated in the wrappings of the child.

Having completed the mural, identifying perhaps with this memorable central image, the artist said: ". . . what I have to say, I say with Sartre, Kafka, Camus . . . 'In the midst of disaster, act as if you could mend that disaster every day.'"[12]

In his essay on James Joyce's *Ulysses* T. S. Eliot wrote:

In using the myth, in manipulating a continuous parallel between contemporaneity and antiquity, Mr. Joyce is pursuing a method which others must pursue after him. They will not be imitators, any more than the scientist who uses the discoveries of Einstein in pursuing his own, independent, further investigations. It is simply a way of controlling, or ordering, of giving a shape and a significance to the immense panorama of futility and anarchy which is contemporary history . . .[13]

These words can apply as well to Lebrun's work. Like Joyce, Lebrun is part of the historical continuum which he altered by his visionary insights and formal power. Growing from a tradition of European painting from which he selected as his paradigms the painters of Pisa's Campo Santo, Ucello, Signorelli, Grünewald, Michelangelo, Caravaggio and the masters of the Italian Baroque, Goya, Blake, Picasso, and Orozco, Lebrun finally found a style completely his own at Pomona. He was able to give up his superb *bel canto* drawing and all mannerisms, saying that drawing "should be, above all, not a thing of art, but a tool for understanding."[14] He gave up color and immersed himself in a world of black and white, a world of darkness, which to him was not only the value of tragedy, but which clarified mass. Black and white also helped eliminate the frills and the unnecessary details, and brought him ever closer to the essence of tactile forms — forms which are, however, constantly metamorphosed and transfigured in accordance with life which is never static. From the *Genesis* mural Lebrun moved on to his cycles on Dante and Brecht and to his immutable and timeless sculptures, which are also related to the great mural, existing as they do in Lebrun's own world located between the actuality of life and the geometry of form.

Notes

1) Rico Lebrun, "About Myself," in *Rico Lebrun Drawings*, Berkeley and Los Angeles, University of California Press, 1961, p. 6.

2) William Ptaszynski, Letter to the author, July 26, 1967. I want to thank Professor Ptaszynski for the indispensable information he supplied about the technical progress on the mural as well as its iconographic meaning.

3) *Ibid.*

4) The progress of the mural on the wall is well documented in a series of photographs by Constance Lebrun and Richard Fish.

5) Martha Davidson, "Rico Lebrun's Mural at Pomona," *Art Journal*, Spring 1962 (XXI:3), p. 174.

6) Rico Lebrun quoted in Elizabeth Poe, "Genesis: Lebrun," *San Diego and Point Magazine*, December 1961, p. 94.

7) Lebrun discusses this problem in a letter of October 12, 1960 to P. J. Kelleher. This letter is printed in *Genesis by Rico Lebrun — Loan Exhibition of Preliminary Sketches for a Mural at Pomona College*, The Art Museum, Princeton University, 1961.

8) Rico Lebrun, in Peter Selz, *New Images of Man*, New York, Museum of Modern Art, 1961, p. 97.

9) *Ibid.*, p. 99.

10) *The Book of Job*, Chapter 18, Verse 7.

11) William Ptaszynski, Letter to the author, July 27-28, 1967.

12) Lebrun quoted in Poe, *op.cit.*, p. 63.

13) T. S. Eliot, "Ulysses, Order and Myth," in Seon Givens, editor, *James Joyce: Two Decades of Criticism*, New York, 1948, p. 201.

14) Lebrun, "Notes on Drawing," in *Rico Lebrun Drawings*, *op.cit.*, pp. 27-28.

Chronology

1900) Rico Lebrun, christened Federico, was born on December 10, in Naples, Italy. Both parents were Italian born, his father Edoardo of French descent, and his mother Assunta Carione, Spanish by heritage. He was the youngest of three children.

1910-1917) In Naples Lebrun attended the National Technical School until 1914, and the National Technical Institute the following three years.

1917-1918) The last year of World War I Lebrun served in the Italian army.

1918-1922) After the Armistice, Lebrun spent two years in the navy. During this time he studied at the Industrial Institute in the daytime and attended free drawing classes at the Naples Academy of Fine Arts at night. He worked with fresco painters Cambi and Albino in Naples.

1922-1924) Lebrun became a designer for a stained-glass factory in Naples.

1924) Early in the year the glass factory established a branch in Springfield, Illinois and Lebrun was sent there as foreman of the factory and instructor in stained-glass technique.

1925-1928) After the expiration of his contract Lebrun moved to New York. He soon became a highly successful commercial artist, ultimately doing advertising illustration for such publications as *Vogue, Harper's Bazaar*, and *The New Yorker*. His first year in New York he met and married Portia Novello, also a commercial artist. Lebrun was supporting his family in Naples, and in 1927 made his first trip back to Italy.

1928-1930) Another trip to Italy was made the following year. At the height of his success as a commercial artist Lebrun began to devote more time to his own drawing, producing a great number of ink studies.

1930-1933) Again, Lebrun went to Italy with his wife, this time to study fresco painting. He worked with Galimberti at the artist's studio on the Via Margutta in Rome. In 1932 he and a fellow student, Louis Rubinstein, went to see the Signorelli frescos on the walls of the cathedral in Orvieto. Lebrun remained in Orvieto for several months to make tracings and sketches.

1933) In January Lebrun returned to New York where he rented a studio on Banks Street. He joined Rubinstein at Harvard University, and together they worked on designs and executed a mural on the top floor of the Fogg Museum. Their work was later walled over.

1934-1935) Lebrun submitted a mural project, "Story of the Mines," to the Guggenheim Foundation. Though this proposal was never executed, he received a Guggenheim Fellowship for 1935/36 on the basis of the preliminary drawings. He began to teach classes in life drawing, mural composition and fresco painting at the Art Students League of New York.

1936-1938) The Guggenheim Fellowship was renewed for a second year. Lebrun began working on a mural for the WPA in Pennsylvania Station Post Office Annex in New York. The mural, "River Flood," was carried out with the assistance of Gridley Barrows, now an architect, and California painter Channing Peake. Conflict arose with the WPA and after two years' work the mural was abandoned, later it was covered over. After the unfortunate end of the post office mural and the breakup of his marriage in 1937, Lebrun left New York.

1938) Channing Peake and his family were instrumental in bringing Lebrun to California. He made his residence in Santa Barbara and accepted a teaching post at Chouinard Art Institute in Los Angeles.

1940) Lebrun married Elaine Leonard in Santa Barbara. He taught animation at Walt Disney Studios. Donald Bear, who came to Santa Barbara to be the director of the newly established art museum, became a source of

encouragement and an influential force in Lebrun's development.

1941) Bear stimulated interest in Lebrun and organized his first exhibition at the Faulkner Memorial Art Gallery in Santa Barbara.

1942-1943) Lebrun was represented in the Museum of Modern Art's "Americans 1942," one of the first important group exhibitions of American painters. He spent a school year teaching classes at Newcomb College for Women, Tulane University.

1944-1945) Julien Levy Gallery gave Lebrun his first one-man show in New York. His work was included in the Museum of Modern Art's exhibition of "Romantic Paintings in America" and in the "American Art Annual" at the Whitney Museum of American Art. Lebrun designed the costumes for the Ballet International's production of *Mute Wife* by Antonia Cobos. His painting, *Bull Ring*, was purchased by the Metropolitan Museum of Art. He became artist-in-residence at the Santa Barbara Museum of Art.

1946) His wife Elaine died.

1947) Lebrun became an instructor at the newly formed Jepson Art Institute in Los Angeles. He won first prize in the exhibition of "Abstract and Surrealist American Art" at the Art Institute of Chicago, and received the Norman Wait Harris Silver Medal. He began work on the *Crucifixion* series.

1948) Lebrun married Constance Johnson, daughter of Pasadena architect Reginald Johnson, and later adopted her son, David. He was awarded first prize at the "Artists of Los Angeles and Vicinity" exhibition at the Los Angeles County Museum.

1950) Lebrun's involvement with the Crucifixion theme was climaxed with the completion of his large "Crucifixion Triptych." The triptych was exhibited at the Los Angeles County Museum, the De Young Museum in San Francisco, and the Museum of Modern Art in New York.

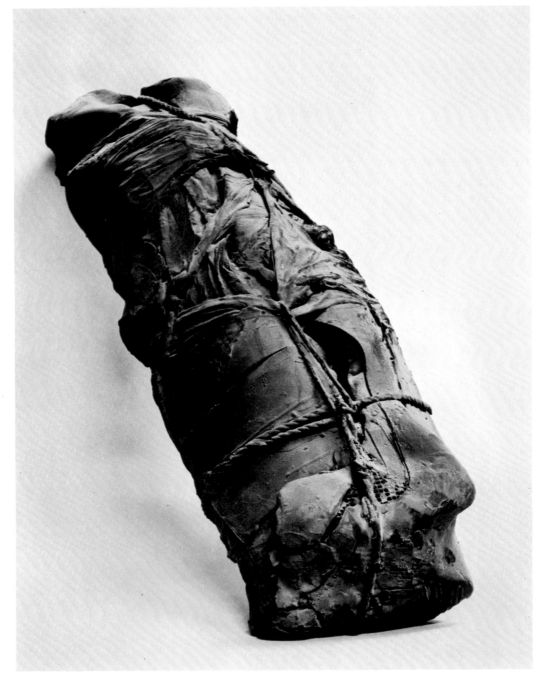

27546

Seven years later the work found a permanent home at Syracuse University. Lebrun made his first trip to Mexico.

1951) The Jepson Art Institute appointed Lebrun director. The Metropolitan Museum of Art awarded him second prize in the "American Painting Today" exhibition. Lebrun did the set and costume designs for Carmelita Maracci's ballet "Circo de España."

1952) Lebrun served on the jury of the "Pittsburgh International Exhibition" at the Carnegie Institute. He was the recipient of the Award of Merit given by the American Academy of Arts and Letters for "outstanding achievement in the past five years in painting." He began a year and a half stay in Mexico, teaching at the Instituto Allende, San Miguel de Allende. Many of the large collages and drawings executed in Mexico were destroyed by Lebrun before he returned to the United States.

1953) A painting from the Crucifixion series brought Lebrun the Pennsylvania Academy of the Fine Arts' Temple Gold Medal.

1954-1958) After his return to Los Angeles from Mexico, Lebrun began work on his Buchenwald series. He taught summer classes at the University of California.

1958) Lebrun spent one year as a Visiting Professor of Art at Yale University.

1959) Lebrun was artist-in-residence at the American Academy in Rome. He was commissioned to do a mural at Pomona College in Claremont, California. Assisting Lebrun on the Pomona mural, "Genesis," were William Ptaszynski, Santa Barbara artist, and James Pinto of San Miguel de Allende.

1960) The National Institute of Arts and Letters elected Lebrun a member. A book of his drawings was published by the University of California Press.

1961) The Pomona mural was completed. Lebrun began his series of drawings illustrating Dante's "Inferno." He made a visit to Japan. In the fall he was invited to participate in the Tamarind Lithographic Workshop program and executed prints illustrating the "Inferno," Bertholt Brecht's "Threepenny Novel," and a "Crucifixion" after Grünewald.

1962) In February he went to Mexico at the invitation of the Nueva Presencia group of painters. Lebrun received his third Guggenheim Fellowship. He was granted the Purchase Award at the Third Biennial National Print Exhibition at the Pasadena Art Museum.

1963) Lebrun became seriously ill and required repeated hospitalization. He began work on a series of sculpture with the assistance of George Goyer. The Pennsylvania Academy of the Fine Arts awarded him the Walter Lippincott Prize.

1964) On May 9, Rico Lebrun died of cancer at his home in Malibu.

Helene Winer

Bibliography

1935
Rico Lebrun. New York: The Art Students League of New York, (1935).

1938
"Rico Lebrun to Teach in California" *Magazine of Art*, vol. 31, no. 12, December 1938, p. 718.

1940
Frankenstein, Alfred. *San Francisco Chronicle*, December 1, 1940.

Pauling, Litti. "Diversity of Mediums and Style Adds Interest to Exhibition at Faulkner"' *The Santa Barbara News-Press*, February 10, 1940, pp. 11-12.

1941
Bear, Donald. "Rico Lebrun" *Pacific Art Review*, vol. 3-4, Winter 1941-1942, pp. 8-13. ill.

"American Paintings and Sculpture" Art Institute of Chicago *Exhibition Calendar*, no. 19, July 17-October 5, 1941, p. 27.

1942
"American Paintings and Sculpture" Art Institute of Chicago *Exhibition Calendar*, no. 23, October 29-December 10, 1942, p. 25.

Frankenstein, Alfred. "An Art in Various Strange Shapes" *San Francisco Chronicle*, May 24, 1942.

Miller, Dorothy C. *Americans 1942: Eighteen Artists from Nine States.* New York: Museum of Modern Art, 1942. pp. 79-85, ill.

1943
Soby, James Thrall, and Miller, Dorothy C. *Romantic Painting in America.* New York: Museum of Modern Art, 1943, p. 183.

1944
Frost, Rosamund. "The Whitney Does it Again" *Art News*, vol. 43, November 15, 1944, pp. 9-10. ill.

New York Times. January 23, 1944, part II, p. 7. Rewald, John, and Wheeler, Monroe. *Modern Drawing.* New York: Museum of Modern Art, 1944. ill.

1945
"38th Annual Exhibition of American Painting" *Bulletin*, City Art Museum of St. Louis, vol. 29, nos. 3-4, 1945.

1946
Bear, Donald. "Santa Barbara Museum of Art marks Fifth Anniversary" *Art Digest*, vol. 20, no. 18, July 1, 1946, p. 5. ill.

Bouchage, Luc. "Louvre to California" *Art News*, vol. 45, no. 8, October 1946, p. 33. ill.

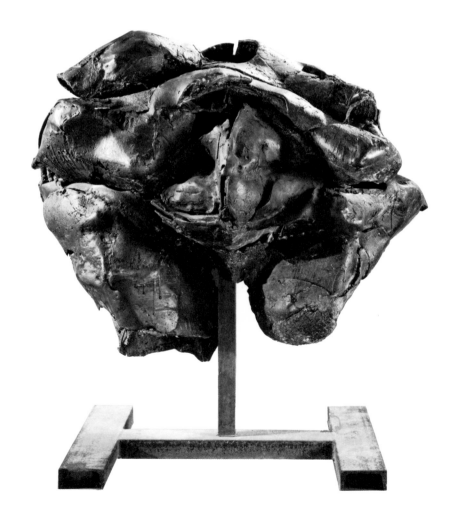

Chase, Edward L. *Intelligent Drawing*.
New York: Coward-McCann, Inc., 1946.
pp. 59-61. ill.

1947
Barefoot, Spencer.
"The Arts Exhibits in Review"
San Francisco Chronicle, August 8, 1947.

Bear, Donald.
"Rico Lebrun Works Reveals
Skill, Strength, Integrity"
Santa Barbara News-Press, July 13, 1947,
part C, pp. 1-2.

Frankfurter, Alfred M.
"Two States of the Union"
Art News, vol. 46, no. 9, part I,
November 1947, pp. 14-16. 60. ill.

Gallery News. William Rockhill Nelson
Gallery of Art, Kansas City,
Vol. 13, no. 7, April 1947.

Genauer, Emily. "This Week in Art:
Chicago Show Proves Abstract Art in U.S.
Stronger than Ever "
New York World Telegram,
November 8, 1947.

"Rico Lebrun Wins Honor
in Chicago Exhibition "
Santa Barbara News-Press,
November 16, 1947, part C, p. 10.

Ross, Kenneth. "Art and Artists:
Distinguished Drawings by Rico Lebrun "
Pasadena Star News, June 15, 1947, p. 21.

"Art News of the Year "
Art News Annual XVIII, 1948, p. 140. ill.

Hess, Thomas B.
"The Whitney: Exhibit Abstract"
Art News, vol. 47, no. 8, December 1948,
pp. 24, 25, 59, 62. ill.

"Lebrun Rated Areas
Artist of Distinction "
Los Angeles Times, September 12, 1948,
part 4, p. 4.
Loucheim, Aline B. "Art in California"
New York Times, August 29, 1949. ill.

M. [Millier], A. [Arthur].
"Crucifixion Drawing
Show Lack of Feeling"
Los Angeles Times, December 26, 1948,
part 4, p. 5. ill.

Millier, Arthur.
"Youth Keeps Southland's Art Display"
Los Angeles Times, May 23, 1948. ill.

Riley, Maude Kemper.
"Art is Everywhere"
Progressive Architecture,
December 1948, p. 8.

1949
Bouchage, Luc. "Lebrun's Crucifixion"
Harper's Bazaar, April 1949,
pp. 142-143. ill.

"Drawings by Rico Lebrun "
Gallery News,
William Rockhill Nelson Gallery of Art,
Kansas City, vol. 16,
November 1949, p. 3. ill.

"Lebrun Drops Grace
for Torturous Force "
Los Angeles Times, December 25, 1949.

Wight, Frederick S.
*Milestones of American Painting
in Our Century*.
New York: Chanticleer Press, Inc., 1949.

1950
"Art" *Time*, vol. 55, no. 24,
June 12, 1950, p. 50. ill.

Bear, Donald. "Lebrun Paints a Picture"
Art News, vol. 49, no. 8,
December 1950, pp. 36-37, 39, 59. ill.

Boyd, E. *Arts and Architecture*,
vol. 67, no. 3, March 1950, p. 8.

Breuning, Margaret.
"Lebrun, Lean but Rich"
Art Digest, vol. 24, no. 13,
April 1, 1950, p. 17. ill.

Bulletin, Philadelphia Art Alliance.
vol. 29, November 1950, pp. 7, 12. ill.

Burrows, Carlyle. "Art Week:
Lebrun Strong in Conviction"
New York Herald Tribune, April 2, 1950.

Devree, Howard.
New York Times, April 12, 1950.

"Exhibition of Drawings and Paintings
of the Crucifixion in Los Angeles"
Art News, vol. 49, no. 8,
December 1950, p. 53. ill.

*First International Biennial of
Contemporary Color Lithography*.
Cincinnati Art Museum, 1950. ill.

F. [Frankfurter], A. [Alfred] M.
"Rico Lebrun's," *Art News*, vol. 49, no. 2
April 1950, p. 43.

Frankfurter, Alfred M.
"Seven Americans Open in Venice"
Art News, vol. 49, no. 4,
Summer 1950, p. 24.

Genauer, Emily. "Americans at Venice"
Art Digest, vol. 24, no. 17,
June 1, 1950, p. 4.

Hale, Robert Beverly.
*100 American Painters
of the Twentieth Century*. New York:
The Metropolitan Museum of Art, 1950.

Langsner, Jules.
"Art News from Los Angeles"
Art News, vol. 48, no. 9,
January 1950, p. 52.

Langsner, Jules.
"Lebrun's Hugh Crucifixion Murals"
Los Angeles Times, December 10, 1950. ill.

L. [Langsner], J. [Jules], and
Boyd, E. "Lebrun"
Arts and Architecture, vol. 67, no. 12,
December 1950, pp. 25-27. ill.

"Major Art Exhibition
Set for Museum Debut "
Los Angeles Times,
November 30, 1950, part 2. ill.

Millier, Arthur.
"Lebrun's Hot Anger against Cruelty"
Art Digest, vol. 25, no. 6,
December 15, 1950, p. 13. ill.

Millier, Arthur. "Los Angeles Events"
Art Digest, vol. 24, no. 8,
January 15, 1950, p. 4.

Millier, Arthur.
"Shock Power Marks Crucifixion Series "
Los Angeles Times, December 10, 1950. ill.

Nine Paintings by Rico Lebrun.
(Introduction by William R. Valentiner),
New York:
Jacques Seligmann and Co., Inc. 1950. ill.

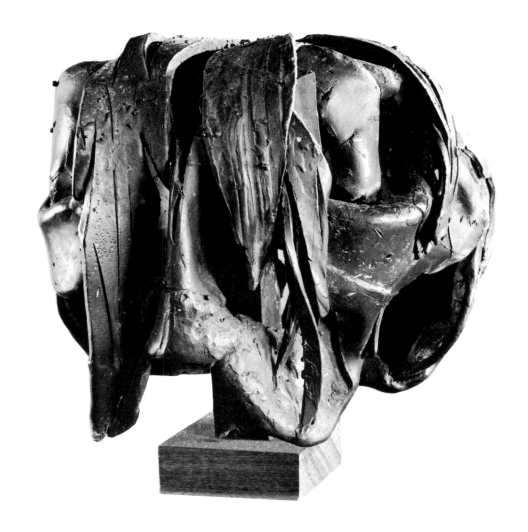

Pearson, Ralph M. "A Modern Viewpoint"
Art Digest, vol. 24, no. 14,
April 15, 1950, p. 6.

Pearson, Ralph M.
The Modern Renaissance in the U.S.A.
Part III "Rico Lebrun." Nyak, New York:
Design Workshop, 1952, pp. 8-13. ill.

*Rico Lebrun: Paintings and Drawings
of the Crucifixion.*
Los Angeles County Museum, 1950. ill.

Ross, Kenneth.
"L. A. County Museum Premiere Timely"
Los Angeles Daily News,
December 9, 1950.

Von Groschwitz, Gustave.
"Full-Color Comeback"
Art News, vol. 49, no. 2,
April 1950, p. 30. ill.

1951
"Art: Big Shocker" *Time*, vol. 57,
March 19, 1951, p. 65. ill.

"Crucifixion Mural by
Rico Lebrun to be Shown"
New York Times, February 22, 1951, p. 29.

P. B. "A Lebrun Profile"
Art Digest, May 1, 1951. ill.

Breuning, Margaret.
"New York Calvary Cycle"
Art Digest, vol. 25, no. 15,
May 1, 1951, p. 17. ill.

Garth, John.
"Art World: Lebrun at de Young"
The Argonaut, November 1951, p. 18.

Genauer, Emily. "Art and Artists"
New York Herald Tribune,
March 4, 1951, section 4, p. 8. ill.

Forty American Painters, 1940-1950.
The University Gallery,
Department of Art,
University of Minnesota, 1951.

Frankenstein, Alfred.
"Lebrun's Crucifixion"
San Francisco Chronicle,
November 4, 1951.
This World Magazine Section, p. 23.

"Museum of Modern Art Shows
R. Lebrun Crucifixion Triptych"
New York Times,
March 4, 1951, part 2, p. 9.

Neumeyer, Alfred.
"Rico Lebrun Hailed as Powerful Artist"
Santa Barbara News-Press,
July 15, 1951, section B, pp. 1-2. ill.

"Portrait " *Art News*,
vol. 49, January 1951, p. 43.

1952
"Academy Merit Award to Rico Lebrun"
New York Times, April 24, 1952, p. 6.

"Artist-in-Residence at Institute Allende
in San Miguel de Allende, Mexico"
Art News, vol. 51, no. 7,
November 1952, p. 7.

O'Connor, J. Jr. "Jury of Award for
1952 Pittsburgh International"
Carnegie Magazine, vol. 26, 1952,
pp. 228-229. ill.

"Rico Lebrun"
Current Biography, Summer 1952. ill.

"Wins 1952 Award of Merit of the
American Academy of Arts and Letters"
Art Digest, vol. 26, no. 16,
May 15, 1952, p. 10.

Seldis, Henry J. "Rico Lithographs"
Santa Barbara News-Press,
November 9, 1952, section C.

1953
Spaeth, Eloise.
"Synthesis of Arts in America:
20 Contemporaries"
The Hindustan Times,
Art Supplement, May 6, 1953.

1954
Goodall, D. B. "Interview with Lebrun"
Art Digest, vol. 29, no. 1,
October 1, 1954, p. 17. ill.

1955
Langsner, Jules.
"Art News from Los Angeles"
Art News, vol. 54, no. 1,
March 1955, pp. 14, 60. ill.

Langsner, Jules. "Rico Lebrun"
Arts and Architecture, vol. 72, no. 2,
February 1955, pp. 12, 13, 38. ill.

Millier, Arthur.
"Lebrun Exhibit Strikes Home"
Los Angeles Times,
March 20, 1955, part 4, p. 8. ill.

Rodman, Selden. *The Eye of Man:
Form and Content in Western Painting.*
New York: Devin-Adair Co., 1955.

Seldis, Henry J. "Los Angeles:
Mexican Impressions at the
Frank Perls Gallery"
Art Digest, vol. 29, no. 7, April 1955, p. 16.

1956
Holland, Frank.
"Colorful Abstract Showing"
Chicago Sun-Times,
January 15, 1956, section 2, p. 5.

Langsner, Jules. "Los Angeles"
Art News, vol. 55, no. 8,
November 1956, pp. 50, 62.

Longo, Vincent.
"Exploration through Collage:
Interview with Lebrun"
Arts, vol. 31, no. 3,
November 1956, pp. 68-69. ill.

Rodman, Selden.
"Conversation with Rico Lebrun"
Art in America, vol. 44, no. 3,
Fall 1956, pp. 33-36, 60. ill.

Rodman, Selden.
"Crucifixion of Rico Lebrun"
Perspectives U.S.A., vol. 15,
September 1956, pp. 69-81. ill.

Seldis, Henry J. "Art and Artists"
Santa Barbara News-Press,
December 9, 1956, section B, p. 6. ill.

Seldis, Henry J.
"Artists of the West Coast —
A Family of Painters"
Art in America, vol. 44, no. 3,
Fall 1956, pp. 37-40. ill.

"Ten Years Selection of Oils, Drawings,
and Collages at Pomona College "
Art News, vol. 55, no. 8,
November 1956, p. 50.

1957
Baur, John, ed. *New Art in America*,
Greenwich, Connecticut:
New York Graphic Society, 1957.

185) SOLDIER   8″ x 1¹/₂″

196) WOMAN WITH ARMS UNDER BREAST   18″ x 6″

Frankenstein, Alfred.
"Rico Lebrun Paintings at
de Young Museum"
The San Francisco Chronicle,
January 30, 1957, section CCCCAA, p. 24.

Freed, Leonard, ed.
Looking at Modern Painting,
New York: W. V. Norton and Co. 1957.

Golson, Lucile M.
"Rico Lebrun et l'humanisme American"
Prisme des Arts, vol. 10,
March 1957, pp. 20-21. ill.

Langsner, Jules. "Rico Lebrun"
Arts and Architecture, vol. 74, no. 6,
June 1957, pp. 21, 31. ill.

Rodman, Selden.
Conversations with Artists,
New York: Devin-Adair Co., 1957.

1958
"Concentration Camps and
Religious Themes Mark
New Lebrun Sketches"
New Haven Register, November 16, 1958.

Duval, Paul.
"Many Modern Artists Can't Draw"
Toronto Telegram, March 8, 1958. ill.

Getlein, Frank. "History in Pictures"
New Haven Register, vol. 138,
November 29, 1958, p. 22.

"Lebrun Cites Moves of Artists"
New Haven Register, November 29, 1958.

Millier, Arthur.
"Death Camps Arouse Artist"
Los Angeles Times,
July 20, 1958, part 5, p. 6.

1959
Bulletin, Philadelphia Art Alliance, vol. 38,
November 1959, p. 11.

Driscoll, Edgar J. Jr.
"From Golgotha to Buchenwald in a Day"
The Boston Globe, April 26, 1959. ill.

"Lebrun's Paintings Speak
Eloquently of Human Form"
Los Angeles Times, March 15, 1959.

"Paintings, Drawings and
Collages at Occidental"
Art News, vol. 58, no. 4, June 1959, p. 60.

Seldis, Henry J.
"Works Apt to be Given More Attention"
Los Angeles Times,
November 1959, part 5, p. 6.

Selz, Peter. *New Images of Man.*
New York:
Museum of Modern Art, 1959.

Taylor, Robert.
"Lebrun Reveals Major Talent"
The Boston Sunday Herald,
May 3, 1959, section 6.

1960
"Art Museum Shows Own Collection
of Lebrun's Drawings"
Santa Barbara News-Press,
November 13, 1960. ill.

Latimer, Ronald.
"The Splendor of Rico Lebrun"
The New Mexican,
February 28, 1960, p. 20.

"Lebrun Inducted as Member of
National Institute of Arts and Letters"
New York Times, May 26, 1960, p. 38.

"Lebrun Named Member of
National Institute of Arts and Letters"
New York Times, February 24, 1960, p. 74.

"Notes and Drawings by Rico Lebrun."
The Massachusetts Review,
Winter 1960, p. 300. ill.

Lebrun, Rico.
Rico Lebrun Drawings.
(Foreword by James Thrall Soby)
Berkeley: University of California Press,
1960. ill.

Rodman, Selden. *The Insiders.*
Baton Rouge: Louisiana State
University Press, 1960.

1961
"Art: Death and Transfiguration"
Time, vol. 77, no. 20,
May 12, 1961, p. 70. ill.

Duval, Paul. "Best of Two Worlds"
Toronto Telegram, April 15, 1961.

"A Talk with Rico Lebrun" *Image 3.*
Summer 1961, Los Angeles:
Student Body of Otis Art Institute, p. 9.

Kessler, Charles S. "Los Angeles,
Bacon, Bloom, Lebrun" *Arts,* vol. 35, no. 4,
January 1961, p. 14. ill.

Langsner, Jules.
"Genesis — A Mural by Rico Lebrun"
Arts and Architecture, vol. 78, no. 9,
September 1961, pp. 16-17. ill.

Lebrun, Rico.
*Rico Lebrun Paintings and
Drawings 1946-1961.*
(Introduction by Peter Selz)
Los Angeles: University of
Southern California, 1961.

Rodman, Selden. "A Mural Enterprise"
New York Times,
May 28, 1961, part 2, p. 14.

Rodman, Selden.
Conversations with Artists.
New York: Capricorn Books, 1961.

Seldis, Henry J.
"Lebrun Genesis Work
Finished at Pomona"
Los Angeles Times, Calendar Section,
January 1, 1961, pp. 18-19. ill.

Seldis, Henry J.
"Long Overdue Exhibit of Lebrun's Finest"
Los Angeles Times, Calendar Section,
April 16, 1961, p. 16. ill.

Strickler, Carolyn.
"Highlight Profile: Rico Lebrun"
Los Angeles Examiner, April 9, 1961. ill.

1962
Davidson, Martha.
"Rico Lebrun Mural at Pomona"
The Art Journal, vol. 21, no. 3,
Spring 1962, pp. 143, 174. ill.

"El Hombre en el Arte de Nuestro Tiempo"
Nueva Presencia 4, April 1962.

Fenwick, K. M. "Rico Lebrun Drawings"
Canadian Art, vol. 19,
May 1962, p. 241.

Lebrun, Rico and Rich, Daniel Catton.
*Illustrations for Dante's Inferno,
Drawings by Rico Lebrun.*
Worcester Art Museum, Massachusetts,
1962. ill.

"Rico Lebrun" *Art News,* vol. 61, no. 8,
December 1962, p. 56.

Wight, Frederick S.
The Artist's Environment: West Coast.
Fort Worth: Amon Carter Museum, 1962.

1963
Henning, Edward B.
"In Pursuit of Content"
Bulletin, The Cleveland Museum of Art,
vol. 50, no. 8, October 1963, p. 234. ill.

Nordness, Lee. ed. *Art USA Now.*
(Text by Allen S. Weller),
New York: The Viking Press, 1963. ill.

"Rico Lebrun" *Art News,* vol. 62, no. 4,
Summer 1963, p. 17.

"Rico Lebrun's 'Brecht' Drawings
to be Shown" *Bulletin,* Philadelphia
Art Alliance, vol. 41, no. 4,
January 1963, p. 7. ill.

Secunda, Arthur.
"An Interview with Rico Lebrun"
Artforum, vol. 1, no. 11,
May 1963, pp. 34-35.

Weller, Allen S.
*Contemporary American Painting
and Sculpture.* Urbana:
University of Illinois Press, 1963. ill.

W. [Wholden], R. [Rosalind] G.
"Rico Lebrun" *Artforum,* vol. 1, no. 12,
June 1963, p. 14.

1964
Ahlander, Leslie Judd.
"Smashing Show Depicts Inferno"
The Washington Post,
January 12, 1964, section G, p. 8. ill.

Ciardi, John, and Baskin, Leonard.
*Drawings for Dante's Inferno and
the Encantadas by Herman Melville.*
Los Angeles: Silvan Simone Gallery,
1964. ill.

Coke, Van Deren.
The Painter and the Photograph.
Albuquerque:
The University of New Mexico Press,
1964. ill.

Howell, Betje. "Perspective on Art"
Evening Outlook, March 13, 1964.

"Muralist Rico Lebrun Dies
at Malibu Home" *Los Angeles Times,*
May 10, 1964, section B, p. 2. ill.

"Rico Lebrun. Artist, 63, Dead:
Expressionist Painted Murals"
New York Times, May 11, 1964. ill.

"Rico Lebrun,
Noted Artist Dies in Malibu"
Santa Barbara News-Press,
May 11, 1964. ill.

S. [Seldis], H. [Henry] J.
"Lebrun In Memoriam"
Los Angeles Times, Calendar Section,
May 17, 1964, p. 25. ill.

Seldis, Henry J. " Rico Lebrun Emerges
as Stirring Sculptor"
Los Angeles Times, Calendar Section,
January 19, 1964, p. 3.

Seldis, Henry J. and Wight, Frederick S.
Rico Lebrun. Newport Beach, California:
Pavilion Gallery, 1964.

Tillim, Sidney. *Arts,* vol. 39, no. 3,
December 1964, p. 70.

"Tribute Paid Artist Lebrun at Services"
Los Angeles Times, May 24, 1964,
section B, p. 6.

"Wanting to Tell the Truth"
Time, vol. 83, January 31, 1964, p. 47. ill.

Wholden, Rosalind G.
"Spectors-Drawn and Quartered"
Arts, vol. 38, no. 9, May 1964, pp. 17-18.

1965
Genauer, Emily.
"Lebrun and Dufy: Pain and Peace"
New York Herald Tribune,
November 7, 1965, p. 47. ill.

Kramer, Hilton.
"Reclaiming the Tragic Element"
The New York Times,
December 5, 1965, part 2, p. 21. ill.

Morosini, Duilio. "Rico Lebrun:
un Maestro dell' arte americana d'oggi"
Paese Sera, February 10, 1965.

1966
Feldman, Edmund B.
Art as Image and Idea. New Jersey:
Prentice-Hall, Inc., 1966.

1967
Hill, Edward. *The Language of Drawing.*
New York: Prentice-Hall, Inc., 1967.
—H.W.

One-man Shows

1940
Faulkner Memorial Art Gallery,
  Santa Barbara, California
San Diego Fine Arts Gallery, California
San Francisco Museum of Art, California

1942
M. H. De Young Memorial Museum,
  San Francisco, California
Santa Barbara Museum of Art, California
San Francisco Museum of Art, California

1944
Julien Levy Gallery, New York

1945
Colorado Springs Fine Arts Center,
  Colorado

1947
Jepson Art Institute,
  Los Angeles, California
M. H. De Young Memorial Museum,
  San Francisco, California
Santa Barbara Museum of Art, California

1948
American Federation of Art, New York
  (organized and circulated)
Modern Institute of Art,
  Beverly Hills, California

1949
Jepson Art Institute,
  Los Angeles, California
William Rockhill Nelson Gallery of Art,
  Kansas City, Missouri

1950
Jacques Seligmann Gallery, New York
Los Angeles County Museum, California
Philadelphia Art Alliance, Pennsylvania
Salt Lake Art Barn, Utah

1951
Frank Perls Gallery,
  Beverly Hills, California
Jacques Seligmann Gallery, New York
M. H. De Young Memorial Museum,
  San Francisco, California
Museum of Modern Art, New York
Santa Barbara Museum of Art, California
Tacoma Art League, Washington

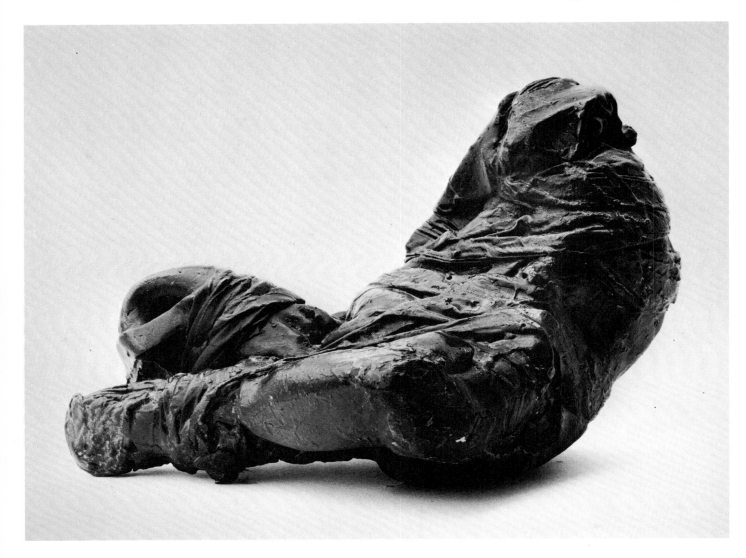

1952
Santa Barbara Museum of Art, California

1954
Colorado Springs Fine Arts Center,
   Colorado

1955
Art Institute of Chicago, Illinois
Frank Perls Gallery,
   Beverly Hills, California

1956
M. H. De Young Memorial Museum,
   San Francisco, California
Pomona College Art Gallery, Claremont,
   California
Santa Barbara Museum of Art, California
Whyte Gallery, Washington, D.C.

1958
De Cordova and Dana Museum and Park,
   Lincoln, Massachusetts
Gallery of Contemporary Art,
   Toronto, Canada
The Art Gallery of Toronto, Canada
University of Utah, Salt Lake City
Yale University Art Gallery,
   New Haven, Connecticut

1959
Boris Mirski Gallery,
   Boston, Massachusetts
Boston University Art Gallery,
   Massachusetts
Occidental College, Eagle Rock, California

1960
Esther Bear Gallery,
   Santa Barbara, California
Santa Barbara Museum of Art, California
University of California, Santa Barbara

1961
Fisher Gallery, University of Southern
   California, Los Angeles
Municipal Art Gallery,
   Los Angeles, California
Princeton University Art Museum,
   New Jersey

1962
Albany Institute of History and Art,
   New York
Associated Artists of Pittsburgh,
   Pennsylvania
Boris Mirski Gallery,
   Boston, Massachusetts

Cornell University, Ithaca, New York
East Cleveland Museum Galleries, Ohio
Joe and Emily Lowe Art Center,
   Syracuse University, New York
Lee Nordness Galleries, New York
Odelisk Gallery, Washington, D.C.
Worcester Art Museum,
   Massachusetts

1963
Boris Mirski Gallery,
   Boston, Massachusetts
Lee Nordness Galleries, New York
Philadelphia Art Alliance, Pennsylvania
Silvan Simone Gallery,
   Los Angeles, California

1964
Colorado Springs Fine Arts Center,
   Colorado
Mickelson Gallery, Washington, D.C.
Lee Nordness Galleries, New York
Pavillion Gallery, Newport Beach,
   California
Portland Art Museum, Oregon
Silvan Simone Gallery,
   Los Angeles, California

1965
American Academy of Arts and Letters,
   New York
Nuova Pesa Gallery, Milan, Italy
Kolver Gallery, Chicago, Illinois
Nuova Pesa Gallery, Rome, Italy
Ohio Wesleyan University,
   Delaware
Pennsylvania Academy of Fine Arts,
   Philadelphia
Silvan Simone Gallery,
   Los Angeles, California

1966
Antioch College, Yellow Springs, Ohio

Group Exhibitions

1939
Whitney Museum of American Art,
New York. "American Art Annual"
(drawings) (following years: 1938, 1939,
1940, 1942, 1943, 1944, 1946, 1947, 1948,
1950, 1952, 1960, 1962)

1940
University of Illinois, Urbana.
"Contemporary American Paintings"
(following years: 1951, 1957,
1959, 1961, 1963)

1941
Colorado Springs Fine Arts Center,
Colorado. "Artists West of the Mississippi"
(following years: 1947, 1948, 1951, 1955,
1956, 1957, 1959)
The Art Institute of Chicago, Illinois.
"Annual Exhibition of American
Paintings" (following years:
1942, 1948, 1951, 1960)

1942
Museum of Modern Art, New York.
"Americans 1942: 18 Artists from
9 States" (also exhibited at the San
Francisco Museum of Art)

1943
Museum of Modern Art, New York.
"Romantic Paintings in America"
The Pennsylvania Academy of the Fine
Arts, Philadelphia. "Annual Exhibition"
(following years: 1951, 1952, 1953,
1956, 1957, 1958, 1960, 1962)

1944
Museum of Modern Art, New York.
"Modern Drawings"
Whitney Museum of American Art,
New York. "American Art Annual"
(painting) (following years: 1948, 1950,
1952, 1957, 1958, 1960)

1945
Carnegie Institute, Pittsburgh,
Pennsylvania. "Pittsburgh International
Exhibition of Contemporary Art"
(following years: 1952, 1955, 1959)
Los Angeles County Museum, California.
"First International Exhibition of
Contemporary Art"
City Art Museum of Saint Louis, Missouri.

"38th Annual Exhibition"
Museum of Modern Art, New York.
"Twentieth Century Drawings"

1946
Colorado Springs Fine Arts Center,
Colorado. "New Accessions USA"
(following years: 1948, 1950, 1952, 1958)
Los Angeles County Museum, California.
"Artists of Los Angeles and Vicinity"
(following year: 1950)

1949
California Palace of The Legion of Honor,
San Francisco. "Annual" (following years:
1950, 1951, 1952)
Institute of Contemporary Art,
Boston, Massachusetts.
"Milestones of American Painting in our
Century" (also exhibited at the Art
Association of Montreal, Canada,
Cleveland Museum of Art, Colorado
Springs Fine Arts Center, Los Angeles
County Museum and M. H. De
Young Memorial Museum, San Francisco,
Los Angeles County Museum, California.
"Artists of California"
Toronto Art Gallery, Canada.
"Contemporary Art in Great Britain,
France, and the U.S.A."

1950
Cincinnati Art Museum, Ohio. "First
International Biennial of Contemporary
Color Lithography"
The Metropolitan Museum of Art, New York,
"American Painting Today"
Venice, Italy. "Venice Biennale"

1951
Los Angeles County Museum, California.
"Contemporary Paintings in the United
States" Brooklyn Museum, New York.
"Revolution and Tradition"
University of Minnesota, Minneapolis.
"40 American Painters"

1952
Albright-Knox Art Gallery, Buffalo Fine
Arts Academy, New York. "Expressionism
in American Painting"

1953
Calcutta University Institute (organized
by ALI-India Arts and Crafts Society
Calcutta, India)
Park Lane House, London. "The
Christian Theme in Contemporary Arts"

Sao Paulo Museum of Modern Art,
Brazil. "2nd International Bienal"
(following year: "3rd International
Bienal 1954")

1954
Musee National D'Art Moderne, Paris.
"Le dessin contemporain aux Etats Unis"
The Art Institute of Chicago, Illinois.
"Masterpieces of Religious Art"

1955
Denver Art Museum, Colorado.
"Annual" (following year: 1956)

1956
Association Francaise d'action artistique,
Paris."Dessins Americains contemporains"
University of Utah, Salt Lake City.
"Survey" following years: 1957, 1958,
Walter Art Center,
Minneapolis, Minnesota.
"Expressionism 1900-1955"
Yale University Art Gallery, New Haven,
Connecticut. "20th Century Drawings"

1957
University of Illinois, Urbana.
"Twentieth Century Works of Art"
Wichita Art Museum, Kansas.
"Paintings by Artists of the West Coast"

1958
Cleveland Museum of Art, Ohio.
Dallas Museum of Fine Arts, Texas.
"Religious Art of the Western World"

1959
Corcoran Gallery, Washington, D.C.
"Biennial" (following years: 1961, 1963)
"New Directions in Painting"
The Detroit Institute of Arts, Michigan.
"2nd Biennial of American Painting and
Sculpture" (in collaboration with the
Pennsylvania Academy of the Fine Arts)
Museum of Modern Art, New York.
"New Images of Man"
The North Carolina Museum of Art,
Raleigh. "Masterpieces of Art,
W. R. Valentiner Memorial Exhibition"

1960
Silvan Simone Gallery, Los Angeles,
California. "The Insiders" (also exhibited
at the Cober Gallery, New York)
University of California, Los Angeles.
"Fifty Paintings by Thirty-seven
Painters of the Los Angeles Area"

1961
Dallas Museum of Fine Arts, Texas.
"Direction in Twentieth Century
American Painting"
Mexico D.F.,
"Pan American Biennale"

1962
Amon Carter Museum of Western Art,
Fort Worth, Texas. "The Artist's
Environment: West Coast" (also exhibited
at the Art Galleries University of
California, Los Angeles and the
Oakland Art Museum)
Art Galleries, University of California,
Los Angeles.
"Lithographs from the Tamarind
Lithography Workshop"
Virginia Museum of Fine Arts, Richmond.
"American Painting"

1963
Mathildenhohe, Farmstadt, Germany.
"Zeugnisse der angst in der
Modernen Kunst"
Providence Art Club, Rhode Island.
"Kane Memorial Exhibition"
Solomon R. Guggenheim Museum,
New York. "20th Century Master
Drawings" (also exhibited at the
University of Minnesota and the Fogg
Art Museum, Harvard University,
Cambridge, Massachusetts)
University of Kentucky, Lexington.
"Graphics"
Sao Paulo, Brazil.
"7th International Bienal"

1964
Otis Art Institute, Los Angeles, California.
"First Biennial Invitational
Drawing Exhibition"
The University Art Gallery,
University of New Mexico, Albuquerque.
"The Painter and the Photograph"

1965
Museum of Art, Carnegie Institute,
Pittsburgh, Pennsylvania. "Exhibitions of
Contemporary Painting and Sculpture"
The Detroit Institute of Arts, Michigan.
"The Johnson Collection of Contemporary
American Paintings"

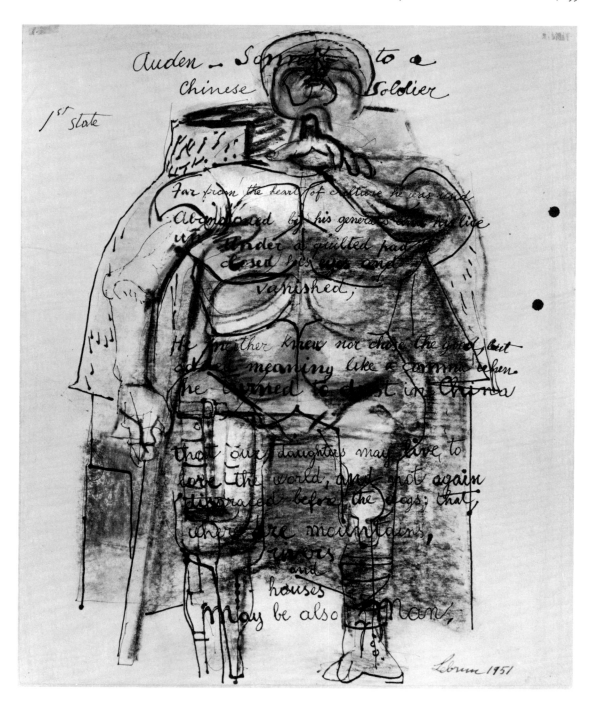

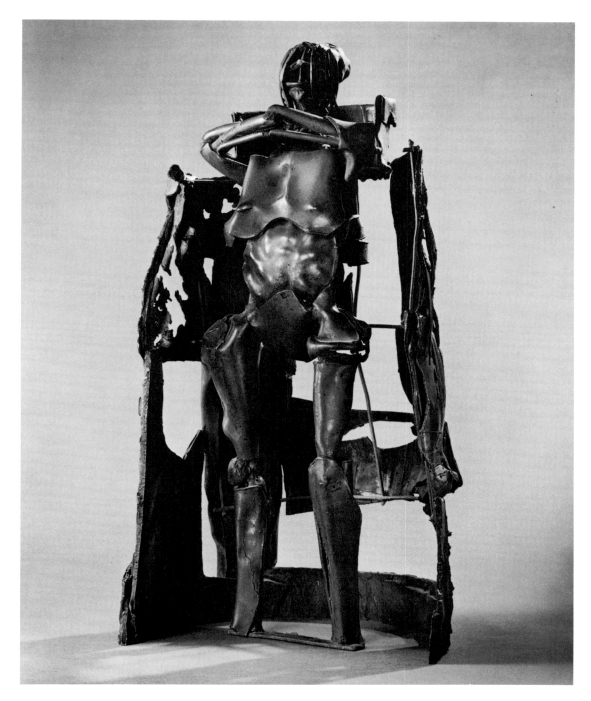

Photography:

Ron Chamberlain
Geoffrey Clements
The Cleveland Museum of Art
Ed Cornachio
Constance Lebrun Crown
Richard Fish
Fogg Art Museum
The Metropolitan Museum of Art
Eric Pollitzer
Santa Barbara Museum of Art
Syracuse University
Worcester Art Museum

Design:
Milton Zolotow

Production:
Lauri Provencher

Typography:
Ad Compositors, Inc.

Lithography:
George Rice & Sons

7,500 copies
November 1967